CONVERGENCE OF ESP WITH OTHER DISCIPLINES

Edited by
Nadežda Stojković
Gabriela Chmelíková
Ľudmila Hurajová

Series in Education

VERNON PRESS

Copyright © 2019 Vernon Press, an imprint of Vernon Art and Science Inc, on behalf of the author.

All rights reserved. No part of this publication may be reproduced, stored in a retrieval system, or transmitted in any form or by any means, electronic, mechanical, photocopying, recording, or otherwise, without the prior permission of Vernon Art and Science Inc.

www.vernonpress.com

In the Americas:
Vernon Press
1000 N West Street,
Suite 1200, Wilmington,
Delaware 19801
United States

In the rest of the world:
Vernon Press
C/Sancti Espiritu 17,
Malaga, 29006
Spain

Series in Education

Library of Congress Control Number: 2018945336

ISBN: 978-1-62273-701-7

Also available:

Hardback: 978-1-62273-429-0

E-book: 978-1-62273-549-5

Product and company names mentioned in this work are the trademarks of their respective owners. While every care has been taken in preparing this work, neither the authors nor Vernon Art and Science Inc. may be held responsible for any loss or damage caused or alleged to be caused directly or indirectly by the information contained in it.

Every effort has been made to trace all copyright holders, but if any have been inadvertently overlooked the publisher will be pleased to include any necessary credits in any subsequent reprint or edition.

Table of Contents

Foreword   v

Preface   vii

CHAPTER ONE
**Designing Writing Materials for
Tourism Text Genres through Technological Tools**   1
M. Angeles Escobar, Iria da Cunha

CHAPTER TWO
**Material Development for *Listening to Financial
and Economic News*: A Case Study**   19
Huang Jian

CHAPTER THREE
**Teaching Medical Geology in English: Research Articles
as a Potential Learning Tool in a University Context**   43
Miriam Pérez-Veneros, Jorge Diego Sánchez,
Elena Giménez-Forcada

CHAPTER FOUR
**Assessment Issues in ESP-Based College English
Program Reform in China's Tertiary Educational
Institutions: A Case Study Of CUFE**   57
Shi Wenjie

CHAPTER FIVE
**Improving Social Competences
of Nursing Students in ESP Classes**   69
Anna Stefanowicz-Kocoł, Monika Pociask

CHAPTER SIX
**Cultural Sensitivity in
Aviation English Communication**　　79
Vanya Katsarska

CHAPTER SEVEN
**The Use of Lexical Bundles in Korean
Learner Corpus – Directions for ESP Pedagogy**　　91
Jungyeon Koo

CHAPTER EIGHT
**Integrating Biblical and Historical Precedent Units
Awareness in Teaching ESP in Terms of Media Discourse**　　111
Svetlana Rubtsova

CHAPTER NINE
**Using English-Chinese Parallel Corpus in
Teaching Translation: A Study on Translator's Notes**　　119
Ting-hui Wen

CHAPTER TEN
**Motivation in Teaching Speaking in ESP:
A Comparison between Two Private
Lebanese Universities**　　137
Wassim Bekai, Samar Harkouss

CHAPTER ELEVEN
ESP vs. CLIL in Higher Education　　157
Gabriela Chmelíková, Ľudmila Hurajová

Contributors　　167

Foreword

Welcome to the collection of essays *Convergence of English for Specific Purposes with Other Disciplines*! This volume, edited by Nadežda Stojković, Gabriela Chmelíková and Ľudmila Hurajová, discloses the variety and scope of research in ESP courses and the design of study materials for different professional fields, ranging from courses of English for tourism to English for aviation, English for medical geology and English for nursing.

The collection opens with Chapter 1, developed by M. Angeles Escobar and Iria da Cunha, which focuses on designing writing materials for tourism text genres using technological tools. Chapter 2 reports on the results of the comparative study conducted by Wassim Bekai and Samar Harkouss on motivation in teaching speaking ESP in two Lebanese universities. Chapter 3 is Huang Jian's contribution which presents a case study on material development for listening to financial and economic news. Chapter 4, developed by Vanya Katsarska, discusses cultural sensitivity in teaching aviation English. Chapter 5 provides Jungyeon Koo's findings of the use of lexical bundles in Korean learner corpus for ESP pedagogy. It is followed by Svetlana Rubtsova's Chapter 6 which considers the use of Biblical and historical precedent in teaching ESP and translation in political media discourse. Chapter 7, developed by Miriam Pérez-Veneros, Diego Sánchez and Elena Giménez-Forcada, analyses the potential of research articles for teaching and learning medical geology in English in a university context. Chapter 8 presents Shi Wenjie's case study on assessment issues in an ESP-based college programme in China's tertiary education. Chapter 9 reports on the results of Anna Stefanowicz- Kocoł and Monika Pociask's investigation into improving social competences of nursing students in ESP classes. Chapter 10 presents the findings of Ting-hui Wen's research on the use of English-Chinese parallel corpus in teaching translation. In the last Chapter, Gabriela Chmelíková and Ľudmila Hurajová discuss the advantages and disadvantages of ESP and CLIL in higher education.

Discussed by scholars from across the globe, this collection addresses interesting theoretical and practical aspects of course and material design in the context of English for Specific Purposes. Enjoy!

Prof. Dr. Nijolė Burkšaitienė
Mykolo Romerio universitetas, Vilnius, Lithuania

Preface

English for Specific Purposes (ESP), but also more generally Language for Specific Purposes (LSP), is in its rationale for existence tied to the discipline whose linguistic, communicative basis it provides. ESP is a form of English Language Teaching (ELT) that performs language training directed towards enabling English language lecturers to design and conduct courses that are solely aimed to enable learners to linguistically function in a target professional domain setting. For that to be achieved, an ESP course is designed specifically for the required environment. In practice this means that an ESP lecturer is to research the professional setting, analyze, abstract and synthesize its linguistic characteristics, e.g., the expert vocabulary, typical syntactic structures, relevant morphological word formation processes, exemplary text organization, both written and spoken stylistics. All this is needed in order to design and/or compile teaching and learning material and decide upon the appropriate teaching methodology and pedagogy so that the course in its entirety simulates that particular professional situation. Only if the course simulates it successfully, will the learners be able to fully and immediately engage into the profession, and through uninhibited communication in the work place, perform their jobs to the benefit of all engaged.

There exist no (or too few) ready-made teaching material or methodological approaches since each professional setting, though undeniably sharing characteristics with the overall domain, is nevertheless unique. A dedicated ESP lecturer caters for those idiosyncrasies doing minute, multifaceted linguistic investigation into the linguistic characteristics of the professional domain. This book is to prove the variety, depth, and quality of the ESP research done into probing the linguistic specificities, and of ESP converging with different professional disciplines.

Nadežda Stojković, Gabriela Chmelíková, Ľudmila Hurajová

CHAPTER ONE

Designing Writing Materials for Tourism Text Genres through Technological Tools

M. Angeles Escobar, Iria da Cunha

Introduction

The area of English for Tourism Purposes is both complex and diverse. Recently, a review and analysis of the most difficult tourism texts has been presented in Spanish in da Cunha, Montané and Coll (2017) and in da Cunha, Escobar, Montané and Fisas (in press). These authors argue that there are robust differences in the perception of their writing difficulties. Also, they show that professionals are also aware of the fact that some genres are more frequent than others. Students need additional help while writing texts that are specifically difficult in this field. The main objective of this paper is to show how teachers can benefit from a semi-automatic writing system that students can use to practice, both individually and with tutors or in groups. In a nutshell, we attempt to give an account of a number of linguistic characteristics, concerning three particular levels: text, lexicon, and discourse, addressing five tourism textual genres that present difficulties for students, those being: promotional articles, travel blogs, reports, tourist accommodation regulations and business plans. By integrating technology, we show how teachers can change the way they usually teach writing for specific purposes. ArText is the semi-automatic writing system employed in our study. This prototype can freely be downloaded from the Internet (http://sistema-artext.com). We draw on the possibilities of this system to engage students in their learning process. In particular, they are presented with a real corpus of texts taken from the Tourism Industry. The texts on the screen can then be analysed in respect to vocabulary, discourse and body content. In this way, technology results in a practical way to teach students how to structure the document, assign titles to the sections, add prototypical content and incorporate linking words and expressions related to the text.

As is well known, visual scaffolding is an excellent way to provide comprehensible input to ESL students. Our main tenet is that students need to learn the key parts of difficult texts in this way. Not only will they learn the essential writing skills for these text genres but they will also make progress in their acquisition of English for Specific Purposes (ESP). Therefore, we attempt to engage students in the learning process increasing their attention and focus, through a meaningful learning experience. First, we consider a semi-automatic writing system to provide a comprehensive description of some text genres to Spanish-speaking students that acquire ESP in a formal context of distance education.

In particular, we want our students to analyse the main aspects that should be included in each of the aforementioned texts in Spanish in order to find their English counterparts addressing text structure, body contents, key phrases, and vocabulary. Section 2 describes some current methodologies in the ESP classroom based on corpus studies and technology. Section 3 provides a description of a new semi-automatic writing system called arText, which may be relevant in this kind of methodology. Section 4 attempts to discuss five textual genres in Tourism following that corpus analysis. Section 5 offers concluding remarks.

ESP and Teaching

New teaching methodologies in ESP have recently been developed in several contexts in tertiary education:

> "(1) *Content-and-language integrated learning (CLIL), (2) use of didactic case studies, (3) corpus studies conducted for teaching purposes and aimed at identifying high frequency language elements: terms, specialized lexis items, collocations, phrases, formulae, acronyms, etc., that need to be prioritized in language courses, (4) more effective coursebooks with higher terminology indexes, (5) extended use of online materials, purposes, and (6) teaching professional culture and non-linguistic skills.*" (Jendrych 2013, p. 46).

A corpus usually incorporates those elements of discourse that are repeated in a language with a greater frequency, cf. Bocanegra-Valle, 2010. The design of an ESP course schedule, work materials and classroom activities should take into account data found in corpus studies including real texts. Likewise, the teacher can give the student access to examples of the current use of the language from which the student will extract some guidelines since they will pay attention to clear templates, cf. Schmidt (1990). Moreover, the knowledge of those words that are used more frequently will facilitate the understanding of the speech. Following Thombury (2002) we assume that the relative frequency of a word turns out to be a key factor in determining its inclusion in a syllabus, provided that the most frequent words express the most frequent meanings in the language.

Many researchers also point out the relevance that the analysis of the corpus has in the process of learning a language in the ESP classroom (Flowerdew & Mahlberg 2009; Gavioli 2005; Boulton 2011; among others). They seem to put forward the thesis that working with a text implies the mastery of technical vocabulary. In particular, Gavioli (2005) supports the twofold claim that corpus work provides students with a useful source of information about ESP language features, and that the process of "search-and-discovery" implied in the method of corpus analysis may facilitate language learning and promote autonomy in learning language use. Furthermore, the presence of technical terms with a higher frequency of use among specialists found in corpus studies will favour their natural acquisition among learners. Naturally, course materials that contain a greater number of frequent terms will be preferable to another one with a smaller number. Finally, the evolution of new technologies can facilitate the classroom methodology based on ESP corpus:

> "Language teaching methodology has benefited, like many other areas of study, from the advantages which IT technology offers to trainers and trainees and which have influenced the manner of devising the presentation of the studied information, as well as its dissemination and evaluation with the result that, at present, ESP methodology is substantially influenced by the computer-based learning strategies" (Caraiman, C. 2014, 916).

Students could be guided and encouraged towards making use of these resources as much as possible since they are used to working with technology, and therefore they might feel more motivated. Today, the ordinary textbook on paper is usually combined with numerous online material available to the student as open courses such as E-xplore Technical English, e-learning platforms such as MOODLE, online publications, online dictionaries, the TechnoPlus program, podcasts, webinars, etc. All this adds variety and dynamism to the learning process (cf. Conroy 2010). In the next section, we will be discussing a new semi-automatic writing system that can be extended to the ESP classroom. By doing so, we will be able to offer students the content of the language closer to its linguistic characteristics, dealing in particular, with the most frequent and difficult text genres in Tourism.

A New Automatic Writing System: arText

The arText system (da Cunha, Montané and Hysa 2017) is an automatic editor that assists the user in the drafting of different textual genres corresponding to three specialized areas: Tourism (Promotional article, Travel blog entry, Report, Norms and Regulations, Business Plan), Medicine (scientific article, review article, scientific article summary, clinical history and academic paper) and Public administration (claim, letter of introduction, complaint, request and complaint). These genres are considered the most frequent and difficult to write in these areas, as demonstrated in da Cunha, Montané, and Coll (2017). The system can be used free of charge online from the following address: http://sistema-artext.com/.

The arText system has three modules. Module 1 allows the user to structure their text according to the selected textual genre. The system shows the prototypical sections of this genre, along with the contents that are usually included in each of them. Also, concrete phrases are offered that can be used to describe much of those content areas. For example, for the genre corresponding to the promotional article, this module indicates that four sections are usually included: Header, Introduction, Body, and Annex. Also, the Body section includes various types of content, such as Photos, Most outstanding characteristics of selected points of interest, Proposal of itinerary or itineraries, Reference to historical facts, etc. And finally, for example, Proposal of itinerary or itineraries has several phrases associated with it, such as 'the route starts in [place]', 'take the route/road', 'at the end of the route', etc. Module 2 allows the user to freely perform the spell checking of the text through the spell checker open source Web Spellchecker Ltd., which the arText system has built-in. Also, this module allows the user to format the text since it includes a format bar with the most usual options (size and typeface, insertion of tables and images, assignment of styles, etc.). Module 3 allows the user to perform a linguistic revision of the text once it is written. This module offers innovative suggestions for improving the text in relation to various aspects related to the lexicon and discourse, such as detection of non-defined acronyms, detection of sentences that are too long, proposal for sentence segmentation, alternative discourse connectors and excessive lexical repetition detection, among others. The information provided in Modules 1 and 3 of the arText system is specific to each textual genre and comes from the analysis of a textual corpus (cf. da Cunha, Escobar, Montané and Fisas, in press). Figure 1 shows a screenshot of the main page of the arText system online editor, where the three modules can be visualized.

Figure 1.1. arText editor

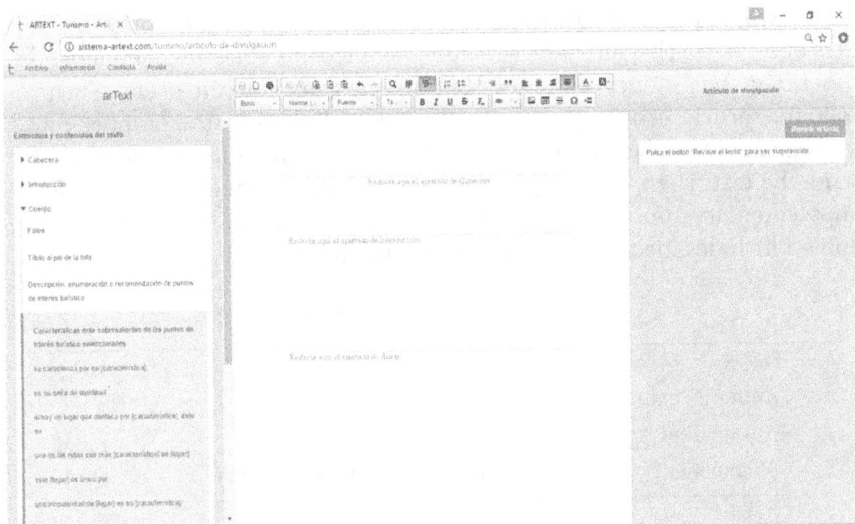

Teaching Tourism Text Genres in English

Writing can be a difficult task in any language, especially when students are writing in a language that is not their first language. After analysing some English texts in the field of Tourism with an English-speaking professor, we attempted to analyse the English counterparts of the most frequent Tourism text genres included in the previously mentioned arText.[1] Let us look into the most important types of genres in Tourism in English and how they are structured concerning three main elements: general overview, the contents found in the body and the main key phrases or vocabulary used in each particular piece of text.

The types of genres that we want to focus on in this paper are: promotional article, travel blog, report, norms and regulations, and business plan. We will see that each of these genres has a specific structure, content, tone, and vocabulary. By introducing all this information to our students, we will be able to make them aware of the importance of using a scaffolding method. The characteristics found in each genre highly depend on the style and tone of each piece of text. In the next pages, we will discuss the relevant elements that usually occur in each of the selected tourist genres in order to offer our students a clear picture of how to cope with the writing of each of these texts.

---

[1] Credit needs to be given to Prof. July Ciancio (Dean of Westcliff Unversity, California) for designing some teaching materials using arText discussed in the text.

Promotional article

When writing a promotional article, students learn to present tourism products or services. The aim here is to help them create professional quality texts describing the product or the service from the general to the useful. The promotional article usually starts with the title, followed by the author's name and the introduction. The introduction shows the intention of the author to write the text. Then, the body has the main promotional content and all the supplementary information can be left for the annexes at the end of the text. Table 1 includes the main structure of the promotion text.

Table 1.1. Promotional Article

- Title
. Author(s) name
- Introduction
. Statement of purpose for writing to the intended audience
- Body
o Photo
o Caption under the photo
o Descriptions, explanations, or **recommendations** about touristic points of interest
o Most salient features of the selected **points of interest**
o Proposed **itinerary** or itineraries
o Background on relevant **historical facts**
o Information about important people associated with the place or point of interest
o Ideas for **activities** or things to do
o Special recognition or prizes awarded regarding the selected points of interest
- Conclusion
- Annexes

As indicated in Table 1, the body contains the most important information, as this is usually the case in most pieces of text. Here one usually includes one or several pictures with a caption underneath that tells us what the picture is about. Then, a number of elements are discussed: descriptions, explanations, or recommendations with touristic points of interest. When someone is trying to promote something, they are trying to encourage people to go and visit that place. One might describe several points of interest or an itinerary that visitors may want to follow. The itinerary is a list of places including a proposed schedule that can be followed while visiting that place. The body might also include historical facts about the area or information on relevant historical people or current citizens that one might find in that place. We could also add activities to do or special prizes that have been given in the hotels or venues to be promoted along with festivals and holidays and places to eat. Logos can also appear in a promotional article providing funding to help promote the place.

Obviously, not all promotional articles need to follow all these elements, since promotional writers have the option to add other elements, although the elements provided above seem to provide the basic skeleton of a promotional article. One should also consider how the information is edited. For example, by using a bold font for the names of the sites to visit or the activities to do, especially when the text is rather long since editing can help to skim through the text to find the most relevant information of that location. The language in the promotional article is usually somewhat friendly since the intention is to encourage people to visit the place. Some of the key phrases that one can find in a promotional piece are as follows:

- This place is characterized by its _____
- Its signature (dish/dance/style) is the _____
- This is a place that is known for its _____

With these sentence frames one can have some flexibility to use different nouns or adjectives according to what needs to be described.

Travel Blog

This is a very common piece of writing nowadays and students may feel they can write them as they are tourists themselves. In fact, many people today write blogs and they do not intend to write about their experiences in a formal style. Rather, they write about their passion for travelling. In other words, travelling stirs up the passion of an individual to start their own blog so that they can share their experiences with others regarding information or insights along with practical tips or suggestions.

As a general outline of the travel blog, one starts with the heading followed by the title. Then bloggers write the introduction with several elements like pictures since they usually have many of them. Note that visual media can easily help bloggers to share their experiences with their own adventurous escapades with the world at large. The most important style that characterizes the travel blog highly concerns the blogger's thoughts. It is about their own reflection on their trip. Therefore, they talk about the reason for wanting to share such pictures with the audience. Table 3 includes the main structure of the travel blog.

Table 1.2. Travel Blog

- Heading
  - Title
- Introduction
  - Photo
  - Captions under the photos
  - Blogger's thoughts (motivation or **reason for writing the post**)
  - Relevant links
- Body
  - **Graphics: photo, photo gallery, videos, maps**
  - Captions under each image
  - **Descriptions, explanations, or recommendations** about touristic points of interest
  - Relevant links
  - Vivid descriptions about **emotions** regarding the traveller's experiences
- Epilogue
  - Conclusion

As indicated in the table above, travellers usually include pictures, visuals, maps, and guides to galleries, among others, in the body of the tourist blog. Relevant captions help their identification so they need to be used as well. There are also many descriptions provided, explanations and recommendations about the sites visited. Recall that the traveller's blog is a personal piece of writing. Hence it is characterized by including many emotions that the traveller wants to express about their trip. However, one can write the blog in the third person with a more impersonal style, although the first person is commonly used to provide the most personal perspective. In any case, the language style in the blog is very informal. It is a personal style of writing and as mentioned before it is very personalized in order to let one's personality come through. In blogs, one can find different topics such as food, history, music, nightlife, etc., as they seem to be exciting for the traveller at one particular point. The most important points of information are also written in bold to draw the reader's attention to all these topics. Exemplary key phrases that characterize blogs are as follows:

- It is incredible!
- It must be a wonderful experience!
- You can see it in all of its splendour!

Note that exclamations are usually found since the author wants to really get their emotions across. Emotive langue is used all over the blog with many adjectives and expressions that can indicate either positive or negative feelings including dangerous experiences, with the intention of providing advice to other travellers about potential risks with the aim to prevent them from dangerous or unwanted situations.

Report

Writing reports is undeniably time-consuming but also an important part of a tourism student's job. They are also an opportunity to discuss tourism issues, since reports usually highlight concerns and also help to communicate the way forward. A report is usually produced by an enterprise, not by an individual, so the tone is very different. It is more serious. It is supposed to be objective, straightforward, and not emotional at all. It is usually written in the third person, with more sophisticated vocabulary. It has a lot of facts, figures, and tables as well as quantitative information.

In the overview of a report, you can usually find a cover page under which there are the logos of the enterprises which are involved either as the companies that try to report on their business or as the companies that provide funding for that particular business. The report usually includes a table of contents. One expects quite a few numbered pages since it is usually very long, around fifteen or twenty pages. This means that it takes some time to write this piece of writing.

As indicated in Table 3 below, the report includes a brief introduction explaining its purpose, the intention and the main audience (ranging from stakeholders, investors, partners or consumers). In the conclusion, one may find a summary of the most important points, and recommendations for actions in the future. Next, some legal disclaimers or confidentiality information can be added. Sometimes the report is produced for internal consumption and therefore it ought not to be used outside the organization. The report ends with the contact information and the company logos.

Table 1.3. Report Overview

- Cover page
  - Title of the document
  - Logos of the enterprises involved
  - Date
  - **Table of contents**
  - Title of the section
  - List of the titles of the sections in the document with their respective page numbers
- Introduction
  - Brief explanation about the main topic of the text
- Body (see Table 4 below)
- Conclusion and recommendations
  - Author's recommendations for the readers
- Legal disclaimers and confidentiality agreement
  - Information about the confidentiality of the text and related information
- Closing
  - Contact information for the authors (individuals or enterprises): name, mailing address, email, etc.
  - Logos of the enterprises involved

As in the previous text genres, the bulk of the information of the report is found in the body, ranging from hotels, hostels, short-stay apartments, locations for leisure activities, vacation notices, among others, as indicated in Table 4. Notice that we might find information similar to that of the promotional article but with more quantitative data, including facts or figures since it is similar to an analysis or evaluation of one or more selected locations. We need to include references to our sources of information and data since it is required to give credibility to the genre. It is also very helpful to make use of some visual support for the reader to remember different pieces of information discussed in the text. Captions should always be used under the graphics or tables. Finally, the end of the body should include some answers to the most general questions regarding objectives, and purpose, which need to be briefly discussed in the introduction.

Table 1.4. Report Body

- Body
▸ Information on the topic: **hotels, hostels, short-stay apartments, hotel networks, locations for leisure activities, vacation services**, etc.
▸ **Analysis and evaluation** of the selected topic
▸ **Quantitative** study data
▸ **References** in the body of the text to the graphical content incorporated into the text
▸ Graphics: photos, images, maps, tables, graphs
▸ Captions under each image
▸ Most relevant answers to the questions posed in the report

Some typical phrases that are found in the report referring to some graphics or pictures are:

- In Graph/Table/Image number XX, you can find _____
- The Graph/Table/Image shows/demonstrates/includes _____
- The aim of this report is to _____
- This report is based on _____

The sentences above usually address the external audience (stakeholders, funders, etc.), with the aim to show them how well the business is doing or trying to keep them investing in the establishment.

Norms & Regulations

When students study tourism management, they need to learn how to write norms or regulations. This text genre is also a long piece of text, which is usually internal or can also be posted for a consumer as well as in the form of legal documentation. For example, norms and regulations in a hotel need to be available to all guests. It is quite objective, and therefore you will not find a lot of adjectives or descriptive language. It is also very straightforward since it regularly acts as a legal document, stating the obligations and rights that need to be followed in one particular establishment. Regulations can appear as numbered items. Table 5 includes the typical overview of this type of text. There are no logos, just a couple of signatures of the directors who are in charge at that particular establishment, with the corresponding contact details. Table 5 includes the typical overview of this type of text.

Table 1.5. Regulations Overview

- Cover page
    - Legal guidelines
    - Reservations
    - Prices
    - Customer payment
    - Cancelations
    - Guest registry
    - Check in and check out
    - Stay
    - Accommodations
    - Hours of operation
    - Additional services
    - Rights, rules, and regulations for clients
    - Pets and service animals
    - Obligations of the establishment
    - Complaints
    - Right to refuse service

The topics that students may find in a piece of Norms or Regulations are highly similar to the topics that they can find in guidelines for making reservations, prices, payment, cancels, etc. The text with regulations usually lets guests know how to keep their own information in the registry, how they should check in or check out, along with other types of information, like the kind of benefits they may receive, among others, as stated in Table 5 above. There are no pictures and no names since the author is not really mentioned. Hence, the use of the passive voice is very common in this piece of text:

- The establishment may request a deposit
- A deposit of $XX is required at the time of booking
- Any modifications to the original booking are subject to availability

With the intention to comply with regulations, this genre needs to offer straightforward information, and refrain from appearing very personal, supporting the main purpose of this text, which is to protect the establishment. Therefore, it usually addresses the staff and the guests since norms and regulations can be used to solve a dispute, among other things. Sentences are quite long, which is typical of what is called "legalese" referring to a legal type of discourse. Given that it is very formal, we usually find expressions that create distance between the authority and the reader. Passive sentences are also very useful as mentioned above, since this piece of text usually addresses the staff in general, and the guests regarding their expectations. Note that regulations can be used to solve a dispute. Hence, everything needs to be clearly stated so as to avoid any kind of legal difficulties in the future.

Business Plan

The business plan is perhaps the most difficult assignment for students. However, this type of text is really useful in the business industry, and therefore students can write business plans for any kind of domain. In essence, this is a very useful genre for anyone who is interested in opening any kind of business. However, each business is unique and, therefore it will differ, among other things, according to the goal, for example, to open an amusement park or a restaurant. The content will also change according to the particular objectives to meet. The overview of a business plan (BP) is also much larger than the previous text genres discussed above. Obviously, there is a lot of information concerning a business plan. Therefore, the writing of this text may involve four steps.

First of all, as indicated in Table 6, a cover page is followed by a table of contents, and by legal and confidentiality information. Then, some background should be included in the introduction providing the particular business context, and then we can go for an analysis of the location considering the place of the proposal to set up the business (country, city, neighbourhood), etc.

Table 1.6. Business Plan Overview I

- Cover page
    - Title of the document
    - Logos of the enterprises involved
    - Date
- Table of contents
    - List of the titles of the sections in the business plan with their respective page numbers
- Legal and confidentiality information
    - Information about the confidentiality of the document and related topics
- Introduction and context
    - Contextualization of the business plan: objectives and general characteristics
- Analysis of the location

- Description of the characteristics of the country, location, city, etc. in which the tourist business is located, key points of analysis of the surrounding conditions and conclusion

The second main section in the business plan should cover the introduction of the sector where some general information is provided regarding its relevance at the moment of writing this project, whether it is booming or it has been recovered in the sector. This part might also include some graphics showing some historical data, as indicated in Table 7. Some analysis of competitors is also useful. Whenever we want to enter into the marketplace, we need to know and identify the main competitors. We should wonder whether there are start-ups in the sector, for example. The analysis of the demand should also be considered. There is no need to go into business if there is no demand for a product or service. Hence one has to show the case as to why this particular business project is important. Notice that the objective of this text is usually to obtain some funding to start the business, and, therefore, it needs to address investors like a bank or a partner, who need to be convinced of the need of starting a new business, which should be put as a brilliant idea.

Table 1.7. Business Plan Overview II

- Introduction to the sector
  - General information about the sector
  - Information about the current state of the sector as well as its history and evolution
  - Graphics
- Analysis of the competitors
  - Description of the characteristics of the main competitors
  - Technical data on the competitors' tourism-related business
  - Information about the strengths and weaknesses of current competitors
  - Graphics: photos, images, maps, tables, graphs
- Analysis of demand
  - Explanation of the segments and characteristics of demand
  - Statistics and data about demand

The third step in the BP writing needs to deal with Strengths, Weaknesses, Opportunities, and, Threats, what is understood as the SWOT analysis, as depicted in Table 8.

Table 1.8. Business Plan Overview III

- SWOT Analysis
    - SWOT in table format
    - Explanation of the model for implementation
    - Information about the structure of the operation and investors
    - Explanation about the expansion strategy
    - Information about the management of the project and the parties involved
- Legal aspects of the project
    - Mention of all legal aspects related to the business plan

Whereas Strengths and Weaknesses are internal to the business, Opportunities and Threats are external since they come from outside, i.e., an opportunity to do something new, and there is usually a competitor. The SWOT analysis can be presented first in a written format as a narrative, and then one can include a table showing each particular element in a more visual fashion with bullet points, helping the reader to find the relevant information at ease, as indicated in Table 8. The model for implementation should also be discussed including a calendar, potential addressees, expansion plans, employment strategy, etc. Then, one should consider the legal aspects, concerning regulations or licenses that need to be obtained, in compliance with tax laws, along with other corporation issues.

Finally, students should look at financial projections as the fourth step in the BP writing, as indicated in Table 9. This is probably the most important part of the business plan. Everything until now has been leading up to this moment. Roughly speaking, the question of how much money one expects to get with this business needs to be addressed, along with other relevant details such as potential funders, budget, expected expenses, etc., since they are very important to show investors that the project is feasible.

Table 1.9. Business Plan Overview IV

- Financial projections
  - Description of the economic aspects of the business plan
  - Detailed budget
  - Tables and graphs
    - Phases and schedule for the project
  - List or graph of each proposed phase in the project
  - Proposed calendar in list form or Gantt chart for the phases of the project
- Conclusion
  - Contact information for the authors (individuals or enterprises): name, mailing address, email, etc.
  - Logos of the enterprises involved

This final part of the BP has a lot of tables and graphs. There is not much narrative style although one needs to explain what those graphs and tables illustrate. Then we go into the phases of the project and here we consider how we will start, what we need to do (buy the property or remodel it) when we develop the webpage, the promotional strategy. All this information can be provided in the so-called Gantt chart that illustrates a project schedule, indicating the start and finish dates of the terminal elements along with a summary of the different phases which sometimes overlap. Finally, the conclusion should indicate the author of the business plan and the person responsible for it, and if a logo is already available, it should also be included.

As mentioned above, BPs are usually long and should also be written in formal style but sentences are usually shorter than the ones found in other formal genres above. It should be written very clearly to make the audience be involved in the future business easily. Among other key phrases that one might find in a business plan, a couple of examples of the type of style are as follows:

- This country is known for its _____
- Tourism in this country is mainly situated in _____
- This project studies the proposal to _____

Conclusions

It is generally assumed that ESP entails designing some learning materials that meet specific needs of students. Technology in ESP can also be very helpful. In particular, we have considered the semi-automatic writing system arText, which is based on a corpus study on the most frequent, and difficult text genres in Tourism. This semi-automatic writing system included a fine-grained analysis of five text genres. Each of them has relevant and particular characteristics related to three linguistic levels: text structure, text contents and key phrases. Students should take these text characteristics into account when they write texts for specific purposes. Therefore, the main goal of this paper has been to provide students with some real English counterparts in order to help them deal with these five text genres in English. In particular, we have presented a scaffolding strategy based on three main elements, namely: structure or overview, body contents and key phrases, all of them to be found in each of the aforementioned text genres: promotional piece, travel blog, report, norms and regulations, and business plan. Our strategy has indicated that these text genres share some specific linguistic characteristics, yet also include other very different ones. These model structures and the linguistic characterization of the five genres analysed can be the basis for instructional materials to learn how to write texts in the field of tourism. Our scaffolding strategy could also be extended to other fields where ESP is involved and where students could also be involved in future research actions by implementing the arText system utilities to other fields.

References

ArText http://sistema-artext.com

Bocanegra Valle, A. 2010. 'Evaluating and designing materials for the ESP classroom'. F. Ruiz-Garrido et al (eds). *English for Professional and Academic Purposes*. Amsterdam/New York: Rodopi. Series: Utrecht Studies in Language and Communication, 141-165.

Boulton, A. 2011. 'Data-driven learning: The perpetual enigma'. In S. Goźdź-Roszkowski (ed.) *Explorations across languages and corpora*. Frankfurt: Peter Lang, 563-580.

Caraiman, C. D. 2014. 'A Practical Approach to the Methodology of ESP Teaching'. 8th International Scientific Session: Challenges of the Knowledge Society. Bucharest: Nicolae Titulescu University Publishing House, 916-922.

Conroy, M. 2010. 'Internet tools for language learning: University students taking control of their writing', *Australasian Journal of Educational Technology*, 26 (6), 861-882.

da Cunha, I., Escobar, M.A., Montané, M. A., Fisas, B. (In press) 'Textual genres presenting writing difficulties in the field of tourism: a semiautomatic corpus-based linguistic analysis'. In Proceedings of the 21st Conference on Language for specific purposes 2017 (LSP 2017). Bergen (Norway).

da Cunha, I., Montané, M. A., Hysa, L. 2017. 'The arText prototype: An automatic system for writing specialized texts'. In Proceedings of the 15th Conference of the European Chapter of the Association for Computational Linguistics (EACL 2017). Software Demonstrations, 57–60.

da Cunha, I., Montané, M. A., Coll, A. 2017. 'Detección de géneros textuales que presentan dificultades de redacción: un estudio en los ámbitos de la administración, la medicina y el turismo'. Revista E-Aesla 3. 352-361.

Flowerdew, J. & Mahlberg, M. 2009. *Lexical Cohesion and Corpus Linguistics.* Amsterdam: John Benjamins.

Gavioli, L. 2005. *Exploring Corpora for ESP Learning.* Amsterdam: John Benjamins.

Jendrych, E. 2013. 'Developments in ESP Teaching. Studies in Logic'. *Grammar and Rhetoric* 34 (1), 43-58.

Schmidt, R. W. 1990. 'The role of consciousness in second language learning'. *Applied Linguistics* 11, 129-158.

Thombury, S. 2002. *How to Teach Vocabulary.* Pearson.

CHAPTER TWO

Material Development for *Listening to Financial and Economic News*: A Case Study

Huang Jian

Introduction

The course in this case study is called *Listening to Financial and Economic News*. It is part of the undergraduate translation program of CUFE (Central University of Finance and Economics, China) which focuses on the translation of financial and economic texts. The graduates of this program are expected to have the potential of offering translation & interpretation services in various fields, especially in the fields of finance and economy. The course *Listening to Financial and Economic News* is offered in the very first year so that the students are given a chance, from the very beginning, to develop their professional identity and confidence, by being exposed to materials that characterize their program. Financial and economic news is selected for the listening materials content as it not only makes up a major part of international news, but it also represents what learners of this program should excel in and be exposed to.

The students, before they are enrolled in this program, have received at least 6 years of English education. They usually have an acceptable general English level but vary greatly in listening comprehension proficiency. This is mainly because importance attached to listening comprehension differs enormously from area to area in China. In some underdeveloped areas, listening is not part of Higher Education Entrance Examination and therefore totally ignored in middle school education, while in the developed areas, especially in metropolitan cities like Beijing and Shanghai, great importance is attached to listening training. The listening test in the first class of this course shows that of all 40 listening items, the best learner gets 28 right and the worst only 3 right. In addition to the wide difference in their listening proficiency, a questionnaire about their past listening learning experiences shows their listening instruction follows the comprehension approach which reduces listening teaching to listening testing (Brown 1990; Vandergrift & Goh 2012). As a result, the learners have very limited declarative and procedural knowledge about listening comprehension. What is more, they have not had a systematic input of finance and economic knowledge, nor translation and interpretation knowledge according to the questionnaire.

Given the specific purpose of the program and the distinctive characteristics of the learners, there seems to be no commercially-produced material available that will fit the course. It thus becomes necessary that proper material should be developed by the teacher specifically for it. With a view to the development, relevant literatures are reviewed in order to find out the ways for selecting the right text and developing the quality tasks. The review shows that a huge number of studies about language learning material have been carried out, producing many principles and suggestions for its development. Yet, few of the studies are focused on listening material development. This is understandable because compared to reading, writing, and speaking, listening instruction is widely and unjustifiably downplayed for it takes place in the hidden reaches of the learner's mind and demonstrable results are hard to achieve by teachers (Field 2008; Nation & Newton 2009). English for Specific Purposes (ESP) listening instruction and its material development, as an emerging branch of listening instruction and material development, suffers even more from the inadequacy of directly relevant research literature. Since there are few specific research results available for guiding the materials development, efforts need be made to develop the materials drawing on relevant studies and to theorize the empirical development process to facilitate future development efforts. This chapter, as a response to the needs, presents (1) the rationales behind the teacher's development of ESP listening materials; (2) students' attitudes to them; (3) a theoretical framework proposed for ESP material development; (4) reflections over the case implications for ESP and material development. It is hoped that the study will benefit those who are interested in ESP listening materials development in terms of both cognition and action.

The establishment of the course goal and objectives

Clearly specified course goal and objectives constitutes a necessary part of both course design and material development. The goal and objectives of this course are established with reference to the existing views of goal and objectives for general L2 listening, ESP L2 listening and the specific context of this course.

Goal and objectives of general and ESP listening instruction

The goal of second language listening instruction is to develop active listeners (Vandergrift & Goh 2012; Goh 2013). Brown (1990, 172) points out that the term "active listener" refers to "someone who constructs reasonable interpretations on the basis of an underspecified input and recognizes when more specific information is required. The active listener asks for the needed information." And Goh (2013, 57) states that to listen actively, language learners need to:

(1) have an available source of relevant knowledge to support cognitive processing;
(2) use listening skills to facilitate comprehension and interaction;
(3) engage in metacognitive processes to enhance and regulate their own comprehension and listening development (Goh 2005; Vandergrift & Goh 2012).

Embedded in such an 'active listener' goal are four broad objectives of knowledge, skills, cognitive processes, as well as meta-cognitive processes for general listening instruction and the four broad objectives can be broken down into many sub-types according to the existing listening instruction literature (Brown 1990; Field 2004, 2008; Vandergrift & Goh 2012; Goh 2013) as shown in Table 1 below.

Table 2.1 Objective type and its breakdown for general listening course

Objective type	Objectives breakdown
Knowledge	Knowledge about the language: phonology, syntax, and vocabulary
	Knowledge about language use: discourse and pragmatic
	Knowledge about context, facts and experiences: prior or background knowledge
Skills	Listen for details
	Listen for main idea
	Listen for global understanding
	Listen and infer
	Listen and predict
	Listen selectively
Cognitive process	Bottom-up (sounds- and text-driven) processing: the decoding of sounds
	Top-down (schema-driven) processing: uses prior knowledge to help listeners draw constrained inferences.
Meta-cognitive process	Planning for the Listening activity.
	Monitoring comprehension
	Solving comprehension problem
	Evaluate the approach and outcomes

As for the goal and objectives for ESP, Goh (2013) maintains that the above-mentioned goal and objectives also apply to ESP listening:

"ESP listening as a construct has many similarities to ESL listening. It involves the same cognitive processes that draw from a number of similar knowledge sources to process spoken input and requires the use of the same core (or "macro") skills that enable effective attention to information in accordance with the purpose for listening. Where the two types of listening differ is in the additional skills and specific types of knowledge required for EAP and EOP purposes" (pp. 57-58).

Goh (2013) continues to point out that though ESP learning materials are typically developed for learners who have roughly an intermediate level of proficiency (McDonough 2010), as far as listening is concerned, some learners might need to work hard to build up their rather low level of listening ability while at the same time learning to develop new skills needed in their specific domains. It is useful therefore to conceptualize ESL and ESP listening development as being interrelated, instead of considering ESP listening development as an 'add-on' to a set of skills that learners already possess. It follows that ESP materials are expected to help learners develop both general English and ESP listening capacity.

Goal and objectives of *Listening to Financial and Economic News*

Having taken into account of the existing knowledge about ESP listening and the specific context of the course in case, the goal and objectives for this course have been formulated as below in Table 2.

Table 2.2 Goal and objectives of Listening to Financial and Economic News

Goal Description	The goal of this *Listening to Finance and Economics News* is to develop active and productive listeners, who can, with inadequate knowledge of various kinds, maximize the understanding of financial and economic news, represent main idea in English, render key sentences into Chinese as well as form their own idea on issues involved in the text.
Objective type	Objective breakdown
Knowledge	Knowledge about the language: phonology, syntax, and vocabulary
	Knowledge about language use: discourse and pragmatic
	knowledge about specific content: personal financing, tax, currency, bank and their connection with the world at large
Skills	Listen for summarizing the main idea
	Listening for interpreting key sentences

	Listening for critical thinking
Cognitive process	Bottom-up (sounds- and text-driven) processing: decoding of sounds
	Top-down (schema-driven) processing: uses prior knowledge to help listeners draw constrained inferences
Meta-cognitive process	Planning for the listening activity.
	Monitoring comprehension
	Solving comprehension problem
	Evaluate the approach and Outcomes

It can be seen from comparison between Table 1 & Table 2 that the goal and objectives set up for this course are different from those for general L2 and ESP listening.

First of all, the goal of developing an active listener is extended or enriched. Section "with inadequate knowledge" is added because L2 listeners, as compared with native listeners, are usually inadequate in both language and relevant socio-cultural knowledge. In this case, learners, as explained in Introduction part, are inadequate to widely different extents in terms of both language and content knowledge. What is most important is that the active listeners in this case, not only need to arrive at a maximum comprehension of the spoken texts but also are expected to be able to represent the main idea and interpret the key sentences. This is added on the ground that the learners in this course are not regular listeners for whom getting information is adequate. They are also potential translators and interpreters who not only need to understand what is said but also need to convey what is said.

As for the specific objective breakdown, prior or background knowledge is replaced with specific content knowledge in order to stress the important role of content knowledge in ESP L2 listening comprehension and its acquisition in this course: leaners are inadequate in it and need to learn it from this course as they learn how to listen. In content knowledge part, 'connection with the world' is added for learners are expected to apply the knowledge they learn from listening course to their real world. The long list of skill objectives has been simplified into three main skills. In addition to 'listening for summarizing and interpreting' which is motivated by the program's specific requirement, 'listen for critical thinking' is added because that is what is expected of all undergraduate learners, which fall into the category of liberal education and should be incorporated into every single undergraduate course. What is more, critical thinking itself is also required for both deep understanding of the spoken text and development of other skills and abilities.

Teacher's initial rationales behind the material development

To meet the above-mentioned objectives, the right materials must be produced. A huge number of principles have been proposed for development of material for general English, a few for ESP and some for ESP listening. With these principles and the particular context of this course taken into consideration, materials have been developed for the course *Listening to Financial and Economic News* based on the Text-Driven Approach proposed by Tomlinson (2003a) which emphasizes the importance of selecting relevant, meaningful and engaging texts to begin with and then developing engaging pre, while-and post-reading (or listening) tasks. The detailed practices and the rationales behind are as below.

Choice of text

For the whole course, a variety of spoken and financial and economic news has been selected mainly from BBC, VoA and other sources. Below is Table 3 showing the texts selected.

Table 2.3 Texts selected for the course

Unit	Text Title
Unit 1: Personal Financing	Lesson 1 value of studying personal finance
	Lesson 2 personal finance for students
	Lesson 3 personal finance for students
	Lesson 4 personal financial planning part 1
	Lesson 5 personal financial plan 2
Unit 2 Tax	Lesson 1 Personal Income Tax System in China Need to Be Changed
	Lesson 2 American Tax Day
	Lesson 3 Japan's consumption tax
	Lesson 4 President Obama Agrees to Extend Tax Cuts for 2 years
	Lesson 5 Evasion of Tax
Unit 3 Currency	Lesson 1 Bitcoin in China: A dream dispelled
	Lesson 2 China's currency undervalued
	Lesson 3 China's currency One way no more
	Lesson 4 China Moves to Internationalize Currency
	Lesson 5 Rigging currency markets

Unit 4 Bank	Lesson 1 Citigroup Paying up and moving on
	Lesson 2 BTG Pactual goes public; Back to basics
	Lesson 3 World Bank and International Monetary Fund Open Spring Meetings in Washington
	Lesson 4 Banking and crime
	Lesson 5 Comerzbank

There, 20 texts were chosen and distributed over 4 units, namely, personal financing, tax, currency, and bank. Clearly, the field of financial and economic news is not confined to these 4 topics and they are chosen as the organizing theme mainly for two reasons: (1) they represent the high-frequency news; (2) there is a systematic content knowledge on each of them which is essential because "Material with a trivial information content, therefore, has low value both as practice material and for motivation" (Morrison 1978,167). The students in this case study are expected to be able to develop proficiency in understanding the news and acquiring content knowledge about these topics. For each topic unit, five relevant texts are selected. Many guiding principles can be found in the literature for choosing spoken texts, such as relevance to learner needs, intrinsic interest of topic, cultural appropriateness, linguistic demands, cognitive demands, logistical consideration, quality and exploitability (McGrath, 2002; Field, 2008). With these in mind and given the specific context of this course, the following considerations are emphasized in text selection.

Topic relevance of spoken English texts

In both language education and translation education, great importance has been attached to topic relevance (Field 2008; Kelly 2012). The merit of students exposed to texts on relevant topics includes graded difficulty, intense content knowledge, and strong motivation. In our selection and organization of texts, special attention has been paid to it. All texts chosen are believed to be relevant to learners to different extents, and we try to move from immediate relevance to remote one on both unit and text level. For example, personal financing is put as the first unit because the first year students have just started to deal with or at least manage their personal financing issue, though, in China, most students are financially dependent on their parents. And within the unit, we put value on studying personal financing before personal financing for students, which then are followed by personal financing for retirement. However, such a move from immediate relevance to remote one is not easy to achieve. As compared with unit 1, the 5 texts of unit 5 are not progressing from immediate to remote as those in unit 1, though the 5 texts all share one single topic that is not far from students' life.

Content knowledge presented in spoken English texts

The role of prior knowledge in facilitating successful L2 listening comprehension has long been established (Long 1990; Chiang & Dunkel 1992). The content knowledge, a special kind of prior knowledge, is stressed based on our view of nature of listening comprehension - prior knowledge matters also in achieving comprehension (Long 1990; Chiang & Dunkel 1992) and our view of listening pedagogy that "listen to learn" (Liu & Miao 2012; Rost 2005)) should be an integral part of listening instruction. There are two main merits of students acquiring content knowledge while listening. For one thing, the accumulated content knowledge will play a role in achieving listening comprehension. For another, being able to acquire content knowledge while receiving listening instruction, like a bonus, will give student richer learning experiences and promote their motivation for learning. Just as mentioned before, the 4 topics are chosen because, for each of them, there is a system of content knowledge behind each. It is hoped that students will be exposed to some key knowledge about each topic at the end of each unit. In order to give students richer exposure to content knowledge, each text is chosen with attention paid to the knowledge points it carries. For example, the second text of unit 2 titled *American Tax Day* is chosen in the hope that learners can get a view of what American individual tax system is like and compare it with its Chinese counterpart that the first text of this unit is about.

Linguistic features of spoken English texts

Listening comprehension and reading comprehension are both receptive language skills. But listening comprehension is distinguished from reading comprehension in that spoken text has linguistic features that do not appear in written texts and are a great challenge for second language listeners (Brown 1990; Field 2008). The listening research literature has offered a long list of these linguistic points which broadly fall into the category of decoding challenges and meaning building challenges (Field 2008). Some features of persistent difficulty for ESP listening has been identified, such as logical connectors, phonology, referential items, nominalized groups, idiom and vocabulary (Morrison 1978). As these features are distinctive for listening comprehension, they should be given priority in text selection. In our case, we do try to choose the texts that carry as many linguistic features as possible, for example, the texts that carry contrast stress and referential items. This is also a response to the fact that our learners have poor listening knowledge. Yet we do not give it the first priority because we organize the texts based on topics rather than linguistic features of spoken texts. In practice, we choose among the texts of a particular topic the ones that carry as many challenging linguistic features as possible.

Graded difficulty

The spoken text chosen should be appropriately graded in order to facilitate the step-by-step progress of the course. However, the grading of texts is hard, especially for spoken ones. The factors that might affect the difficulty, as revealed in current literature, include topic familiarity, content knowledge load, and linguistic features as mentioned above. In this case, the grading of difficulty is first carried out through unit order. The units are organized in the order of immediate relevance of a topic to learner's life. For example, personal financing is closer to students' life than tax and therefore placed in front of it. Secondly, they are organized from easier content knowledge to more challenging content knowledge. Thirdly, the speech speed is also considered. Such factors as text length and lexical difficulty are given less attention because it is hard to find 5 texts for a particular topic which progress from easy to difficult in terms of lexis, syntax, and length, etc.

Development of task

For each text, a sequence of instructional tasks over 3 stages have been developed as shown in Table 4 below:

Table 2.4 Tasks developed for the course

1. Pre-listening Tasks	
1.1	Brain storming questions
1.2	Vocabulary
2. During-listening Tasks	
2.1	Students listening to the text for the first time and trying to write down its main idea as they understand
2.2	Teacher reconstructing the main idea based on students' understanding together with students
2.3	Students listening to the text for the second time as teacher leads for better understanding of the main idea
2.4	Student polishing the main idea based on 2.1, 2.2 and 2.3
2.5	Teacher sharing his version of summary
2.6	Students listening to key sentence chosen by teacher for interpretation
3. After-listening tasks	

3.1	Self-checking: What content knowledge have I learnt? What language knowledge have I learnt? What listening and interpreting skills have I leant?
3.2	Self-reflection: What does financial independence mean to you?
3.3	Development of MC questions

Specifically, 11 sub-tasks are developed for the three stages of instruction process: two sub-tasks for the pre-listening stage, six for during-listening stage and three for the after-listening stage. The rationale for behind the three stages of tasks is explained as below.

Rationale behind pre-listening tasks

The pre-listening stage is designed to prepare students for real listening in terms of both content knowledge, language and affection. The pre-listening stage, in this case, consists of two sub-tasks: brainstorming question and vocabulary task.

The brain-storming question is related to the theme of text chosen. The learners will be given 5 minutes to search for information on the internet and prepare their answer. At the end of the 5 minutes, the learners need to report their answer to their desk-mate within 1 minute. And then the teacher will single out 1 or 2 students to report his or her desk-mate's answer to the class. To finish this sub-task, the student needs to search for information, organize it into an answer, report his own idea, listen attentively to his or her desk-mate and memorize and represent their idea. It is believed that this task can help learners in terms of language, idea, and affection. For language, it allows the learner to use words associated with the topic which may occur in listening; for idea, it activates the topic knowledge and possibly raises questions and expectations about the content to be heard; for affection, it might stimulate the curiosity about what will be heard. What is more, even in terms of process authenticity of listening, the brain-storming part as a warm-up activity is justified: "A listener begins to construct a discourse representation from the very beginning of a listening encounter. But even before the encounter, a wise listener attempts to predict what will be said, in terms either of the ideas that will be mentioned or of the words that are likely to be used" (Field 2018: 260).

Vocabulary task takes the form of giving learners a list of words that will appear in the spoken texts and 3 minutes to familiarize themselves with before the real listening. Two kinds of words are chosen for the list. The first is the kind that learners have difficulty figuring out the meaning from context, and the second is key technical terms related to the topic. Certainly, the two kinds of words sometimes overlap in practice. Judging from the view of listening comprehension process, the vocabulary task is far from being authentic. But seen from the process of interpretation, this task is quite authentic in that an interpreter is preferably given enough time to acquire both content and language knowledge about the particular topic before the work starts.

Rationale behind during-listening tasks

During-listening part is made up of 6 sub-tasks which are focused on training two key skills: summarizing spoken texts and interpreting spoken sentences. The final purpose of sub-task 2.1-2.5 is to help students to construct the main idea of spoken text. It is the key ability both for regular academic profession and translation profession. In regular academic life, students need to be able to get the main idea of oral academic communication taking place from time to time. What is more, as a potential translator, the learners need to be even more skilled at making summary than regular academic learners, for accurate summary is the pre-condition for accurate interpretation. What is more, summary is also a special form of professional translation task (Reiss 2014) besides being a listening pedagogical task. Each sub-task from 2.1 to 2.5 has its own function to serve. The purpose of sub-task 2.1 'first listen' is to train students' ability to immediately process the information retained in their working memory and give students a rough idea of where they are in their listening comprehension proficiency. The sub-task 2.2 of teacher's reconstruction of main idea based on students' understanding is to show students how world knowledge and logic can help them extend their comprehension based on the limited information they can retain in their mind, deepening the learners' understanding of the top-down process of L2 listening. The 2.3 teacher-led listening for the main idea is to show learners where they should pay more attention and that the listening skills and strategy can be used to figure out the text structure, which will also hopefully, build learners' discourse knowledge needed for listening comprehension. Sub-task 2.4 is designed for students to organize in their language the idea they have acquired via the previous tasks. The last sub-task of teacher sharing summary is intended to communicate to learners the success criteria or what a good summary is like, which is one of the most important formative assessment strategy (Black & Wiliam 1998; Carless 2011).

The second skill focused on in the during-listening stage is interpretation. Interpretation is a distinguished new task for listening instruction that is absent in both international testing paper and traditional listening textbooks. This task is intended to train students' ability to listen and transfer between two languages. For this purpose, sentences with listening challenges and interpretation difficulties are chosen. For example, sentences are chosen with pronouns that cause extra trouble to both comprehension and interpretation given the differences between Chinese and English in pronouns usage. In doing the sentence interpretation, students are given the chance to develop their bottom-up decoding skills and the ability to use context and co-text for understanding. Pedagogically speaking, this interpretation task serves the following functions. Firstly, it helps teacher train student's listening skill and strategy. As the interpretation task is based on single sentence and teacher can replay it in such way as to call students' attention to word segmentation, parsing, intonation, etc., and offers a chance for making use of the meaning-building strategies. Secondly, it can train inter-language transfer ability which is required for translation majors and prepare them better for coming translation and interpretation courses, producing an extra advantage in terms of collaboration between different courses. Thirdly, interpretation can serve as a formative assessment task. It is to the advantage of any instructor to have a close understanding of what goes on in the minds of second language listeners, and of the processes in which they engage. Interpretation can help the teacher to elicit more information about not only learning comprehension but also expression problem. When a student gets stuck or fails in the interpretation, the teacher can ask the student what he or she was thinking, which will reveal either listening weakness or transference difficulty and then give feedback accordingly. In this sense, interpretation offers an opportunity for the teacher to identify students' problem and offer ways for improvement.

Rationale behind after-listening tasks

The after-listening stage is designed to help learners reinforce and expand what they have learnt so far. It is done by thinking, writing and discussing without listening to the text chosen. For this course, the after-listening stage consists of three sub-tasks, namely self-checking, self-reflection and multiple choice (MC)-development.

Self-checking sub-task serves the similar function as reviewing task, to push learner to go over what they have learned in the instruction. And it is made clear to students that it is about what they have learned instead of what teacher has taught or stressed. Therefore, it can vary from learner to learner, giving learners a chance to learn to be responsible for their own learning.

In self-reflection sub-task students are encouraged to think, write and speak for their own personal ideas about the key issue(s) involved in the spoken text. As far as comprehension is concerned, the above-mentioned processes are only aimed at textual or literal understanding. However, comprehension is more than that. Adams & Patterson (2008), in exploring reading comprehension, propose three levels of understanding: literal understanding, critical understanding, and effective understanding. These three levels of understanding can well apply to listening comprehension too. Field (2008, 243) has pointed out that: "… Listeners are not simply recorders of information. They make judgments about the information they receive: they select some, they omit some and they store some in reduced form. We should expect the same utterance to result in differently constituted messages in the minds of different listeners." He has also suggested that: "We need to provide practice exercises where learners report not what is said but on its implications." (Field 2008, 238) To expand on this idea, a listener is supposed to not only have a good understanding of what is said but also produce a critical and effective response to what is said. The self-reflection part is designed to give students an opportunity to create such multi-layer responses. In doing the task, students are expected to: develop their critical thinking ability by forming their own idea and use the language and idea they have learned in the listening process. By involving students in doing these, students will also have a better comprehension of the text and have a better real-world motivation for listening. Usually, in the after-listening part, students are asked to work on linguistic aspects of the recording: "The final post-listening phase is often cursory, focusing mainly on new vocabulary or on checking answers." (Field 2008, 83) The self-reflection task takes the 'post-listening' part beyond linguistic level.

The development of MC questions is designed with a view to preparing students for the listening tests they might take in the future. MC questions remain very popular testing items in both domestic and international listening test. In this course, we do not offer MC exercises, as students need training in it. To meet this need, instead of developing quality MC questions which is not easy at all and too much burden for the teacher, learners are encouraged to develop the MC questions based on the spoken text learned and their experience and knowledge about MC. The teacher will discuss with learners the quality of MC questions they developed, helping them to think like a testing item writer. In doing these, in addition to listening skills trained by doing MC questions exercises, students are expected to: improve the test-taking skills and assessment literacy, as well as the skill of writing short and precisely.

As it is seen from above, one of the obvious characteristics of these tasks is that though listening is traditional receptive skill, productive tasks have been developed for its instruction. This advantage of such productive tasks in listening programs can be listed but is not confined to:

(1) It gives teachers more chance to identify students' problem and give feedback.
(2) It agrees with the integrated approach to teaching listening.
(3) It promotes task authenticity and learning motivation.

With all these tasks completed, students are expected to have a thorough understanding of the texts and develop their various language skills (listening, writing, interpreting) skills and thinking ability at the same time.

Students' attitudes to the materials

This section aims at revealing how students are responding to the materials developed. All 20 students in the case are asked to finish a questionnaire about the material used in this course. The questionnaire consists of three parts: (1) the attitudes towards 4 topics chosen; (2) the attitudes towards the text chosen; (3) the attitudes towards the task developed.

Students' attitude towards the four topics chosen

To find out students' attitudes towards the topics set up for this course with the view to figuring out the topic they like most, students are asked a close-ended question: of the 4 units, which is your favorite unit topic, and an open-ended question: why?

For the first question, the findings are as below in Table 5:

Table 2.5 The order of topics favored by students

Topic most favored.	Personal Financing	Tax	Currency	Bank
Number of students	13	1	0	7

As shown above of the total 20 students surveyed, 13 choose 'personal financing" as their favorite topic unit, 7 bank and 1 tax[1].

For the second question, three topic qualities are found contributing to the students' favor and put in Table 6 in order of importance.

Table 2.6 Topic qualities stressed in order of importance

Topic quality favored	No 1	No 2	No 3
	Closeness to Life	Practical Knowledge	Theoretical Knowledge

Obviously, the topic "personal financing" has the largest majority's favor thanks to 3 qualities associated with the topic. The number 1 quality is 'closer to life' (or has immediate relevance to life). "Closer to life" is the phrase used by all 13 students to describe the topic in the very beginning of their explanation. The second quality is that it carries with itself the knowledge (both con-

---

[1] The total student number is 21 because one student picks both tax and bank as his favorite topic.

tent and linguistic knowledge) that can be directly used in their life. For example, one student says: "In contrast with the other three topics that seem more theoretical, personal financing offers knowledge more useful for my personal life, especial in making personal finance decision." Another student puts it as: "Personal financing is close to life and yet I don't know how to talk about it in English. This topic learning gives a lot of English to express what I know in Chinese."

In addition to personal financing, there are 7 students choosing "Bank" as their most favorite topic. However, this topic is favored for different reasons. The students stress the knowledge expansion as the most important reason for loving this topic. Just as one student puts it: "Although bank is just around in our life, we don't actually know much about it. The learning experience of this topic has expanded and deepened my knowledge of bank such as current situation of western bank, categories of bank and function of bank." Of course, this bank knowledge is different from the personal financing knowledge in that it can't be used directly in making personal decision. Yet such more theory-oriented knowledge (or pure pleasure of knowing) can also be appealing to students' mind.

In summary, 2 major qualities contribute to students' favor for a particular topic: closeness to life and knowledge base expansion. And the knowledge can be roughly divided into practical knowledge (both content and language) and theoretical knowledge. Judged by the number of students who vote for their favorite topic, the priority of topic qualities goes as: (1) closeness to life; (2) practical knowledge (joy of using); (3) theoretical knowledge (pure joy of knowing).

Students' attitude towards the text chosen

To understand students' attitude towards the texts chosen with a view to finding out what are the text qualities that the students value, the students are asked to grade each of the text from 0 to 10 points and explain the advantages and disadvantages of each text as listening material. Generally speaking, the students are content with the texts chosen for the course. The average point of all texts is 8.39 with the lowest average text points at 7.95 and the highest at 9.99. And there are 9 of 10 tasks whose average points are over 8. And a closer look at students' view of advantages and disadvantages of each text shows that the students like to judge a spoken text in two broad terms of text content and text language which are broken down into different aspects as shown in Table 7 below:

Table 2.7 Text quality criteria used by students

Breakdown of text quality by students				
Content quality			Language quality	
Knowledge Category	World vs. Subject		Language Input	rich
	Practical vs. theoretical			Interesting
Knowledge Depth	Informative		Discourse Structure	Clear
	Analytic			Complete
Knowledge Attributes	Interesting		Skills points	Listening skill
	Difficult			Interpreting skill

    The knowledge category refers to the different kinds of knowledge contained in the text. In this course, the knowledge mentioned by students can be divided into world knowledge and subject knowledge as well as practical and theoretic knowledge. Knowledge depth refers to whether the text-only presents information or also carry out the analysis of information. Knowledge attributes refer to whether the knowledge involved is interesting or difficult to understand. The rich input refers to the input that carries plenty of new useful expressions, while interesting input the one with some funny or impressive expressions. Students seem to care much for the structure of the spoken text, and they prefer text clearly and completely structured. The students also favor those texts which contain the skills with which to facilitate the listening and interpreting process.

    The most highly rated texts are those which are good in several aspects mentioned above or are quite striking in one or two aspects. On the other hand, those rated lower are those which are not quite good or even poor in one or two aspects and ordinary in other aspects.

Students' attitude towards the tasks developed

To understand students' attitude towards the tasks developed with a view to finding out what are the task qualities that the students value, the students are asked to grade each of the tasks from 0 to 10 points and explain the advantages and disadvantages of each task as listening material. Overall, the students are content with the tasks developed for the course. The average point of all tasks is 8.86, with the lowest average task points at 8.43 and the highest at 9.45. And there are 10 of 11 tasks whose average points are over 8.5

points. Compared with the texts selected, students are more content with the tasks developed. Students like to judge the tasks in broad terms of skills trained, knowledge reinforced and engagement involved, specifically shown in Table 8:

Table 2.8. Task quality criteria used by students

Skill trained	Searching information
	Decoding
	Meaning-building
	Summarizing
	Interpreting
	Critical thinking
	Self-reflecting
	independent learning
Knowledge reinforced	Language knowledge
	Content knowledge
Engagement involved	Immediate response pressure (forced to think)
	Intrinsic affective connection (willing to think)

The skills trained refers to the skills that are developed as the students try to perform the tasks. The knowledge reinforced refers to the knowledge that the students will revisit or apply when they are working on the tasks developed. The engagement involved refers to what extent the task can engage the students. The task is usually engaging in two ways. Some tasks allow student no chance for distraction, such as the task of interpretation where students have to think and organize their language immediately. Another task may not ask students to produce a response immediately, yet is interesting in itself to the students who are encouraged, free from external pressure, to think over it, such being a self-reflection question. For example, there are some students suggesting that more class time should be spent on the discussion of self-reflection task. There are also some students complaining that some warm-up questions are not relevant to the text content and not worth thinking and discussing.

The most highly rated tasks are those which are good in several aspects mentioned in Table 8. On the other hand, those rated lower are not quite good or even poor in one or two aspects and ordinary in other aspects.

Establishment of Course Objectives

Establishment of objectives is the first step of material development as part of course design. However, the objective part is often absent or downplayed in the process of ESP material development. This is probably because the goal of learning ESP is usually thought to be given or agreed as "to use English in a particular domain" (Paltridge & Starfield 2013, 2). But such a goal is too broad and abstract to be informative and instructive for both text selection and task development. What is more, for some courses, the objectives are expected to go beyond the use of English. An objective part is added to this framework to remind the material developers of the fact that: (1) the development process should be guided by the course objectives; (2) informative and instructive objectives might not be given and it is their job to formulate the specific objectives for their own course material; (3) as the double-headed arrows shows, the objective part should be consulted and revised in the whole process of ESP material development. This coincides with the view that course content is something that should be frequently negotiated between teacher, the student and the class as the course unfolds (Holme 1996).

As for the objective breakdown, it can be seen that effective objective is stressed and made visible in this diagram in parallel with knowledge, skill and (meta) cognition mentioned before. The effective objective requires that the course learning experiences help the learners develop a positive feeling towards the course subject and course learning. In response to this, many material development studies point out the need to create effectively engaging material for language acquisition (Masuhara 2006; Tomlinson 2003b). This is because without effective and cognitive engagement there is little possibility of deep processing (Craik & Lockhart 1972) and "deep processing comes from personal involvement as an individual human being" (Tomlinson 2012, 164). Therefore, comprehension questions should be written to elicit localized and personalized responses (Canagarajah 1999). As a matter of fact, affection has been taken into consideration in the material development of this course. For example, the design of self-reflection task is informed by two interrelated sources of knowledge: the stress on effective engagement in material development and the emphasis on deep comprehension in listening instruction. We did not make it visible in the course objectives in Table 2 for two reasons: (1) the affection objective is not well-stressed and listed in the literature about listening instruction objectives; (2) it is not thought independent of other kinds of objectives: considerations regarding knowledge, skill and cognition can contribute to it. However, the students' feedback and the case material development experience show that it matters so much that it deserves to be put at least in parallel with other objectives so that the developers are reminded of its importance and takes it into consideration in every step of material development.

The visible base of ESP material development

The visible development procedure starts with the topic set, proceeds to text selection and ends up with task development. Usually, the material development for language course consists of two steps of selecting right text and then based on text chosen develops quality tasks (Tomlinson 2003a). Yet in this case study, the procedure starts with the topic set. In other words, before text selection, the teacher needs, first of all, to decide the topic category under which the spoken texts will be chosen. Very little discussions can be found in ESP literature on topic set since the topic of ESP material is normally thought to be the same as the specific field where the language is used.

But it is argued from this case that the topic setting step is important and necessary especially for such broad domain as economics and finance. The domain of economics and finance are so big that it consists of many different sub-fields. The practice of setting up a specific topic and then finding texts on it has at least two advantages for text selection: (1) it narrows down the scope of selection; (2) the purpose of ESP becomes more specific, offering representation of a more specific way of language use and a more systematic content knowledge. The text selection and task development of this case are common steps shared by all kinds of language learning material development and are supposed to be carried out with reference to the general principles and the specific context of the ESP listening materials.

The Invisible base of material development

As mentioned before, there is a huge number of principles proposed for material development of which only a small part is specifically for ESP material and listening material. However, the case study shows that in practice, material development is not a process of simply and directly applying these principles. There are so many principles proposed that it is impossible to create the material that fits all principles and the real process involves the teacher developer making and justifying their choices and compromises in the process, which is going on in their mind and is therefore invisible. In simple words, the case study shows that under the process of topic set, text selection and task development there is teacher's invisible choice-justification process and this process is actually based on teacher's belief of what is the right text and task for the students in the specific context.

Such a belief is formed by interaction between teacher's existing theoretical knowledge and empirical findings about the students' needs for and response to the material developed. In this case, this belief is informed by the existing theoretic knowledge about material development. It is suggested by Mackay & Mountford (1978a) that in the design of ESP courses, sociological, linguistic, psychological and pedagogical factors should be taken into consideration. In developing the materials, such factors have been considered. What is different is that the linguistic and pedagogical factors are those closely associated with English listening of which the knowledge comes from researchers on listening instruction. It is proposed that consideration should not be confined to the existing knowledge from literature. The empirical findings of each specific case should be incorporated, especially students' special needs for and their attitudes towards the material developed. This is because each case represents a different learning context, requiring a distinctive material response. Students' attitudes have an impact on how they learn and can reveal the problems with the material (unintentionally) ignored by the developer.

The disadvantages of ESP material development

It has been pointed out that challenge for ESP material development is summarized as the problem of "how to make usable learning instruments from unedited texts in the target language which contain in natural form the important, frequent and useful phonological, lexical and grammatical elements of the target language" (Morrison 1978, 165). But the case study shows that greatest challenge seems more to be finding quality "unedited texts" than to make "usable learning instruments" from them. With differences between ESP and general ELT mentioned above comes a key disadvantage or challenge facing the ESP listening material development: the tension between limited source of linguistic data and a wider scope of instructional expectations. Spoken text is expected to carry specific linguistic features that impact listening comprehension. A wide range of comprehension difficulties associated with linguistic features of spoken texts have been identified in both general English listening studies and ESP listening studies (Field 2008; Morrison 1978). However, it is far from easy to find texts covering the challenging linguistic features identified by empirical studies from a narrower source of data than what is available for general ELT. The students are supposed to be exposed to as many linguistic features as possible that could be challenging to students. However, the narrower source of financial and economic news as compared with general English adds great difficulty to finding the spoken texts with such features. What is more, for ESP material, linguistic data is not only the carrier of language knowledge but also the carrier of content knowledge and it is also expected to be interesting as a learning motivator. The texts meeting so many expectations are definitely harder to collect from a comparatively narrower source.

The advantage of ESP material development

ESP material is usually developed for a small group of learners to prepare them for a specific profession or vocation linguistically. As material of this kind has limited number of users and therefore a limited amount of profits, they are often developed by individual teachers for their students. "The ESP instructor is often perceived to be 'a provider of materials – selecting material that is available, adapting it as necessary and supplementing it in order to meet learners' needs" (Dudley-Evans & St John 1998, 185). This reality, however, constitutes a special advantage for ESP material development: the developer can better cater for the local needs by making full use of whatever is possible in the specific local context. For example, interpretation task seldom appears as a task in international listening materials. For one thing, it is regarded as an evil strategy that should be avoided by learners (Vandergrif & Goh 2012). For another, interpretation requires the teacher master two languages and have some interpretation or translation knowledge while the students also speak the two languages. However, interpretation is used in this case course. "Translation of particular kind can be a useful pedagogical tool in an EST program" because "the information from reading English text is required to be at his disposal in his L1" (Mackay & Mountford 1978[a], 13). It can be seen from here that the legitimacy of a pedagogical tool depends on its utility for language learner in his or her particular context. It is partly in this spirit that the interpretation task has been developed for this listening course, for the students taught are translation majors. They not only need to be able to understand the spoken text but also produce a decent rendition in their mother tongue. And in this case, both the teacher and learners speak English and Chinese, making it feasible to use interpretation as a pedagogical task. This indicates that in developing ESP materials, individual teachers are allowed to integrate all resources suitable for their own class.

Material development as a process of compromise

According to Mackay & Mountford (1978b), compromises of various kinds (academic, linguistic, pedagogic, personal) operate at all levels of course design and the reconciliation of different linguistic and extralinguistic viewpoints and situational demands is integral to the professional role of EST practitioner and an essential aspect of any language teaching operation. Such an observation is well echoed in the process of material development in this case. Theoretically, there are many principles and considerations proposed for material development while practically the developer has to make many compromises in the process of it. It can be seen from this case that: 1) the more objectives the material is expected to serve, the more compromises the developer needs to make; 2) material development seems to be an art of compromise and the quality of materials developed seems to depend on the level of art by which the developer makes the compromises in his or her specific situation; 3) all the principles proposed in the literature from different studies, are better treated, in practice, as reference or inspiration for material developer rather than rules that must be obeyed. What is more, the developer is advised to share with the users the rationale behind material development, including its advantages, limitations and the compromises made in its development so that the users can have a reasonable expectation of it, make a well-informed use of it and make up for its weaknesses by drawing on other materials.

Conclusion

Material development constitutes an essential part of the work for ESP instructors and an important aspect of ESP knowledge base. This case study presents the material response to learning needs for a specific undergraduate program aimed to prepare potential translator with strength in financial and economic texts. And to contribute to the knowledge base of ESP and its material development, teacher's rationales are revealed; students' attitudes are analyzed; a theoretic framework for ESP material development is established, and self-reflections are made. Such contributions, made on the basis of a case study, can be used, hopefully, as reference and inspiration for further practice and research efforts related to ESP material development.

Acknowledgement

This research is supported by the "The State Scholarship Fund" (CSC NO. 201706495030), 2017 CUFE Teacher Development Center Fund (Project No. 040950317001), 2016 CUFE SFS Instruction Methodology Research Fund (Application of Formation Assessment in College English Listening Instruction) and 2014 CUFE SFS Key Academic Research Project Fund (Undergraduate Translation Program from perspective of Professional Translation Program).

References

Adams, W. R., Patterson, B. 2008. *Developing Reading Versatility (10th edition)*. Boston: Wadsworth Publishing Co.

Black, P., Wiliam, D. 1998. Assessment and Classroom Learning. *Assessment in Education*, 5(1), 7-71.

Brown, G. 1990. *Listening to Spoken English*. London: Longman.

Canagarajah, S. 1999. *Resisting linguistic imperialism*. Oxford: Oxford University Press.

Carless, D. 2011. *From testing to productive student learning: Implementing formative assessment in Confucian-heritage settings*[M]. New York: Routledge.

Chiang, J., Dunkel, P. 1992. The effect of speech modification, prior knowledge and listening proficiency on EFL lecture learning. *TESOL Quarterly* 26, 345–374.

Craik, F., Lockhart, R. 1972. Levels of processing: a framework for memory research. *Journal of Verbal Learning and Verbal Behavior* 11, 671–684.

Dudley-Evans, T., St John, M. J. 1998. *Developments in English for Specific Purposes: A Multi-Disciplinary Approach*. New York: Cambridge University Press.

Field, J. 2004. An insight into listeners' problems: Too much bottom-up or too much top-down? *System* 32: 363–77.

Field, J. 2008. *Listening in the Language Classroom*. Cambridge: Cambridge University Press.

Goh, C. C. M. 2005. Second language listening expertise. In K. Johnson (ed.), *Expertise in Second Language Learning and Teaching*. Basingstoke, UK: Palgrave Macmillan, pp.64–84.

Goh, C. C. M. 2013. ESP and Listening. In B. Paltridge & S. Starfield (eds.), *The Handbook of English for Specific Purposes*. West Sussex: John Wiley & Sons, Ltd.

Holme, R. 1996. *ESP ideas*. Essex: Addison Wesleuy Longman Limited.

Kelly, D. 2012. Text Selection for Developing Translator Competence: Why Texts from the Tourist Sector Constitute Suitable Materials. In C. Schaffner and B. Adab (eds), *Developing Translation Competence*. Shanghai: SFLEP, pp.157-167.

Liu, L., Miao, R. 2011. *Theory and practice of L2 language listening* [M]. Beijing: Foreign Language Teaching and Research Press.

Long, D. R. 1990. What you don't know can't help you. *Studies in Second Language Acquisition* 12, 65–80.

Mackay, R., Mountford, A. 1978. The Teaching of English for Special Purpoes: Theory and Practice. In R. Mackay & A, Mountford (eds.), *English for Specific Purposes*. London: Longman, pp.2-21.

Masuhara, H. 2006. The multi-dimensional awareness approach to content teaching. In J. Mukundan (ed.), *Focus on ELT materials*. Petaling Jaya: Pearson/Longman, 1–11.

Morrison, J. 1978. Designing a Course in Advanced Listening Comprehension. In R. Mackay & A, Mountford (eds.), *English for Specific Purposes*. London: Longman, pp.161-179.

McDonough, J. 2010. English for specific purposes: A survey review of current materials. *ELT Journal* 64: 462–77.

McGrath, I. 2002. *Materials Evaluation and Design for Language Teaching*. Edinburgh: Edinburgh University Press.

Nation, I.S.P., Newton, J. 2009. *Teaching ESL/EFL Listening and Speaking*. London: Routledge

Paltridge, B., Starfield, S. 2013. Introduction. In B. Paltridge & S. Starfield (eds.), *The Handbook of English for Specific Purposes*. West Sussex: John Wiley & Sons, Ltd, pp. 1-5.

Reiss, K. (2014). *Translation Criticism-The Potentials and Limitations*[M]. New York: Routledge.

Rost, M. 2005. *Teaching and researching listening*. Beijing: Foreign Language Teaching and Research Press.

Tomlinson, B. 2003a. Developing principled frameworks for materials development. In B. Tomlinson (ed.), *Developing materials for language teaching*. London: Continuum, pp. 107-129.

Tomlinson, B. 2003b. Humanizing the coursebook. In B. Tomlinson (ed.), In B. Tomlinson (ed.), *Developing materials for language teaching*. London: Continuum, pp. 162-73.

Vandergrift, L., Goh, C. C. M. 2012. *Teaching and Learning Second Language Listening: Metacognition in Action*. New York: Routledge.

CHAPTER THREE

Teaching Medical Geology in English: Research Articles as a Potential Learning Tool in a University Context

Miriam Pérez-Veneros, Jorge Diego Sánchez, Elena Giménez-Forcada

Introduction

The establishment and implementation of the European Higher Education Area (EHEA) has aimed at strengthening the interdisciplinary teaching and the quality assurance of higher education. The implementation of English for Specific Purposes in degrees such as Engineering, Law or Medicine was a niche targeted to include real content together and enact real communicative situations that are correlative with the future circumstances that the student may encounter as well as part of the syllabus of other modules in the degree. The Spanish law for Higher Education approved in April 2007 (Spanish Ministry of Education "Organic Law 4/2007" / "Ley Orgánica 4/2007") highlighted this necessity to pair contents, tasks and students' performance based on supplying tools and knowledge to develop skills demanded or expected in future professional situations.

This chapter unveils the strategies and elements designed, implemented and used within an English for Specific Purposes (hence ESP) elective course taught in the Degree of Medicine at the University of Salamanca during the academic year of 2016/2017 under the gracious sponsorship granted by the Vice-Chancellor for Teachers and Innovation in a competitive process that funded Projects for Teaching Innovation. The aim of that project was threefold: firstly, to reinforce the importance given to the implementation of oral skills and self-assessment of students prior to activities of evaluation and, secondly, the integration of an ESP course within the disciplines taught in the degree. Thirdly, it sought to create materials and databases in the elective course "Technical English for Medicine" (which gathered 48 students in their fourth, fifth and sixth years) to create activities that could be used in a mandatory ESP course, "English for Medicine", in the same degree in the fourth year (which comprises a much bigger audience, around 230 students).

The approach granted by the Content and Language Learning (hence CLIL) was the theoretical framework through which the design of the modules aimed at guaranteeing the real context and content of the academic syllabus, therefore reversing the tendency of the subject in previous years and that was not based on real situations. Following the theoretical background provided by CLIL (Ball and Kelly 2015; Coyle, Hood and Marsh 2012; Fortanet-Gómez 2013; Marsh 1994, 2000; Marsh, Pérez Canado y Raez Padilla 2015) the project gathered four specialists in ESP and four experts from the medical background. The first part of the team designed Rubrics for Assessment (both used for self-assessment by students and assessment by the teacher) and tried to contextualise the real situations proposed by the second team, that of experts. This latter section of the project assembled two of the most popular disciplines within the degree, dermatology and oncology, and two incipient areas within Medicine, medical geology, and rheumatology. The course was structured within a simulated International Conference for Young Medicine Researchers, and the students had to present and work together with one of the experts in two oral presentations (work in progress introduction and academic presentation of research) and a research article (RA henceforth).

This paper fosters the teaching potential of RAs for ESP in the scientific realm, with focus on the teaching of vocabulary in Medical Geology (hence MG), as both an emergent and incipient field of knowledge in both the realms of medicine and geology through the use of RAs on MG, which will be hereby analyzed by using corpus-based techniques (Tognini-Bonelli 2001). Since previous work (Diego Sánchez, Pérez-Veneros and Elorza 2017) confirmed that the use of research articles in different fields of knowledge such as dermatology, rheumatology, oncology or medical geology proves an effective and fruitful methodology for teaching (based on the students' surveys and questionnaires), this comparative analysis between RAs written by experts in the field of medical geology and RAs written by students belonging to the degree in Medicine from the University of Salamanca is described in this chapter to assess knowledge about MG and use of scientific jargon and structural patterns with the purpose of communicating science within the scientific community standards. We believe that MG is an adequate field of knowledge because it was a new discipline for students and it is of crucial importance to raise awareness on the issue and its interconnection with other areas of Medicine and also between Biomedical Sciences and Earth Sciences, offering a wider vocabulary.

Medical Geology as an emergent field of knowledge

The composition of rocks and minerals is imprinted on the air that we breathe, the water that we drink, and the food that we eat (Centeno et al. 2016; Bundschuh et al. 2016). Medical Geology (MG) is the scientific discipline that deals with the impact of natural geological materials and processes on the health of individuals. MG intends to correct the lack of knowledge that exists about the interaction that the natural environment plays on the wellbeing of people, increasing the importance of knowing this interrelation and its study in the biomedical and geo-scientific scientific community (Sellinus et al. 2005). MG seeks to stimulate a greater collaboration between both fields of knowledge. This bridge of relationship between disciplines of knowledge so different offers a very suitable field to develop the learning methodology.

It is necessary to bear in mind that many of the elements that the human organism requires are present in the environment and its deficit or excess can generate different health deficits. Medical students can integrate in their learning MG as a new field of science that urges them to recognize health problems associated to the environment from a new point of view: that of the geological environment. The incorporation of MG into the students' training (using English Language learning as tool) can broaden and incorporate factors such as geological variables in the analysis of a disease. A good example of this relationship between geology and human health is the study of health problems caused by high concentrations of arsenic (hence As) in groundwater. Early-life exposure to As is associated with increased risk of cancers found in bladder, lung, liver and urinary tract, as well as cell carcinoma and diabetes (Smedley and Kinniburgh 2002; Bundschuh et al. 2016).

Naturally occurring As in groundwater exceeding the legal limit to be considered potable has been reported in many areas around the world (see RAs by experts which have been used for this study). The MG experts in the project chose these three RAs (Finkelman et al. 2001; Smith et al. 2000; Smith and Hira Smith 2004) which focus on the presence of As in Bangladesh and which state that arsenic is a ubiquitous element widely distributed in the environment and highly toxic in its inorganic form. The other proposed paper (Giménez-Forcada et al. 2017) illustrates how high levels of inorganic As are naturally present in groundwater in a number of countries, including Argentina, Chile, China, Mexico, Bangladesh, India and the United States, and it poses a problem in a growing number of areas. Students could, therefore, relate to a new discipline and yet trace the interaction of factors and the development of an analytical awareness that could be used in the future in the process of deciding clinical verdicts.

The research article: Characteristics and structure

Myers (1990, 1994) describes the RA as a narrative of science since it follows the argument of the scientific community, organizes events as happening simultaneously in time and the vocabulary and syntax used serve the purpose of accentuating the conceptual structure associated to the research field (Myers 1990, 142). RAs focus on the methodology and the procedure followed more than on the outcome of the research itself.

Hyland (2010) states that the research article is also characterized as being written for a specific type of audience, in this case, the scientific community, with its own characteristics. In addition, the research article makes use of specialized vocabulary, technical terminology (see Pecman 2014), nominalizations, acronyms, etc. As Muñoz (2015, 27) asserts, scientists present their findings through the research article so that they can discuss the procedures and the methodologies followed with the rest of the scientific community, thus engaging in scholarly debate and, as a result, constructing new knowledge.

Regarding the structure of RAs, in general terms, they all present a title, an abstract summarizing what the RA will be about, and an introduction to the topic. This is followed by a section in which the materials and methodological steps taken are addressed. This section thus concurs with the assertion of RAs being focused on the methodology followed and the materials used more than on the results or the outcome of that methodology and analysis. Results obtained from the research or experiments carried out constitute the next section of RAs, with a subsequent discussion of those results and conclusions on the investigation. A list of references is equally mandatory as part of its basic structure since the research presented in the RA needs to be based on previous research and needs to have a rooted and sufficiently studied theoretical background on which new scientific knowledge is construed. This list of references also implies that the previous knowledge stated in the RA derives from authorized sources who laid the foundations of the new research, thus avoiding plagiarism. Furthermore, the new research, based on those foundations, aims at filling the gap(s) still existing in the previous research. This gap-filling activity is essential to construe new scientific knowledge and to advance in the development and improvement of the scientific sphere.

Focusing on the description of the research article and the main features which define its nature, students can acquire new scientific knowledge and develop their written skills if this text-type is used as a learning tool in the classroom, also learning scientific jargon regarding different areas of knowledge, in this case, MG. In order to prove our claims, a subsequent comparative analysis between a series of RAs on medical geology and students' research papers was carried out.

The study: Corpus linguistics at work

Previous studies have focused on the usefulness of corpus linguistics and corpus linguistics methodologies for the study of language in academic settings (Thomas and Hawes 1997; Thompson and Tribble 2001) and also for the study of the language used in scientific texts (Hunston 2013). Corpus linguistics accounts for variations in the frequency of appearance and use of both lexical and grammatical terms, also providing the analyst with data on the configurations of grammar and lexis which are more probable to co-occur than others (Hunston 2013, 635). The use of this quantitative approach to the analysis of RAs on MG will shed light on the structure followed in both the experts' RAs and the students' together with a compilation of scientific jargon in this text-type. Furthermore, the fact that previously established categories are used in order to analyze the corpus compiled makes this study corpus-based (Tognini-Bonelli 2001), since the data obtained from the research articles included in the corpus serve to refine these aforementioned categories. The corpus tool used, AntConc (Anthony 2014), generates wordlists which can be later compared to obtain results on the feasibility of the use of RAs to teach MG in English.

What follows is a presentation of the steps taken in the study of RAs written by experts and those written by novice writers:

- Compilation of a specialized corpus of RAs on MG to present students with both the structure of RAs and wordlists with the most frequent words appearing in those RAs. As Muñoz (2015) acknowledges, the compilation of small specialized corpora serves the purpose of producing wordlists which are discipline-based and which specifically suit the needs of students. The texts comprised in this corpus were retrieved from different scientific journals and were the ones used in the course "Technical English for Medicine".
- The experts' RAs were analyzed in terms of their structure for a later comparison with the structure of the RAs written by novice writers. This was done to tackle the question of whether students followed the patterns presented in class to properly and accurately structure an RA.
- The technical words related to MG were also accounted for in terms of the different kinds appearing (types) and their frequency of use (tokens). This was done to carry out a comparative analysis between the technical words used by experts in RAs and those used by non-expert writers in the RAs chosen from the ones elaborated in the course "Technical English for Medicine".

The same steps described above were taken to analyze the corpus of RAs written by the students of the degree in Medicine from the University of Salamanca, considering that writing a research paper was one of the tasks they had to carry out in order to pass the chosen ESP courses in Medicine (in this case both the optional module 'Technical English for Medicine" as well as the mandatory "English for Medicine").

Once the two corpora were analyzed in terms of the structural patterns followed and the technical words (scientific jargon) used, a comparative analysis was carried out to check the validity and feasibility of the use of RAs for the teaching of MG as an emergent but otherwise essential field of knowledge.

Results

This section elaborates on the results of the most frequently used words which are related to the field of medical geology in both the RAs written by experts and those written by students of the degree in Medicine. Furthermore, the section also presents a comparative analysis of the structure followed in the experts' RAs as compared to those from novice writers.

The tables which follow present data related to both the rank and the frequency of use of the word. The term rank refers to the position occupied by the word in relation to the rest of words which make up the article, while frequency indicates the frequency with which the word is used in the article(s) under analysis. It needs to be pointed out that the words selected for the study are those words which are considered as loaded with 'lexical' meaning, as opposed to those conveying 'grammatical' meaning. Words with 'lexical' meaning are those ones which refer to entities in the real world, while 'grammatical' words have no real meaning, such as prepositions, conjunctions or determinants. Hence, the ranks presented in the tables make reference to the position occupied by words with lexical meaning only. Data also relate to the total number of word types (the different types of words found in the articles) and the word tokens (the frequency with which each word type appears in the corpus of articles compiled).

- Research articles written by experts (4 texts) about the contamination of water by As and its effect on human health:

Word types: 4140

Word tokens: 21140

Table 3.1: Rank and frequency of the first 11 terms on As and its effects

Rank (out of 4140)	Frequency	Word
9	202 (0,95%)	**Arsenic**
12	184 (0,87%)	**Water**
26	77 (0,36%)	Health
30	71 (0,33%)	Drinking
35	66 (0,31%)	Concentrations
36	65	Samples
41	56	Exposure
48	48	Skin
52	46	Groundwater
54	45	Cancer
61	42	Wells

Only the first 11 more frequently used terms were taken into account since the frequency of use of term number 12 was quite low (<30 tokens) as compared to the high frequency of use of the terms presented in this study.

- Research articles written by novice writers (2 examples) about the contamination of water by As and its effects on human health:

Article 1: Treatment of chronic arsenic poisoning

Word types: 652

Word tokens: 1721

Table 3.2: Rank and frequency of the first 11 terms on As and its effects

Rank (out of 652)	Frequency	Word
4	46	**Arsenic**
9	27	**Water**
12	16	Drinking
14	15	Skin
19	11	Chelation
23	10	Cancer
25	10	Lesions
28	8	Treatment
29	8	Urine
31	7	Chronic
33	7	Exposure

Article 2: Health effects result in exposure to arsenic-contaminated water, a current behavioural and educational research of the population in Bangladesh

Word types: 598

Word tokens: 1657

Table 3.3: Rank and frequency of the first 11 terms on As and its effects

Rank (out of 598)	Frequency	Word
2	56	**Arsenic**
7	36	**Water**
11	17	Health
12	16	Cancer
13	15	Drinking
14	14	Exposure
15	14	Skin
17	13	Contaminated
23	11	Concentrations
28	9	Contamination
29	9	Groundwater

- Combined data of the two research articles written by novice writers:

Word types: 1030

Word tokens: 3378

Table 3.4: Rank and frequency of the first 11 terms on As and its effects

Rank (out of 1030)	Frequency	Word
4	102 (3%)	**Arsenic**
8	63 (1,85%)	**Water**
13	31 (0,9%)	Drinking
14	29 (0,85%)	Skin
15	26 (0,77%)	Cancer
17	23	Health
23	21	Exposure
24	19	Contaminated
25	19	Lesions
28	15	Concentrations
44	11	Chelation

The two most frequent terms in the case of the four research articles analyzed are *arsenic* (x202) and *water* (x184). They occupy rank 9 and rank 12, respectively. Turning our attention to the first research article written by students, again the two most frequent words are *arsenic* (x46) and *water* (x27), presenting rank 4 and rank 9, respectively. The second article written by students again has *arsenic* (x56) and *water* (x36) as the two most frequently used words (rank 2 and rank 7, respectively). Finally, if we study the two articles written by students in combination to obtain information about the frequency and rank of scientific words, results point to the fact that, invariably, *arsenic* (x102) and *water* (x63) are again the two most frequent words, with a 4 and an 8 rank, respectively.

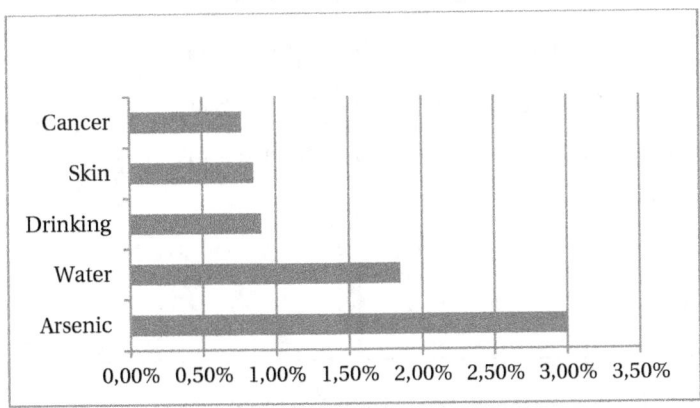

Chart 1. RAs written by experts

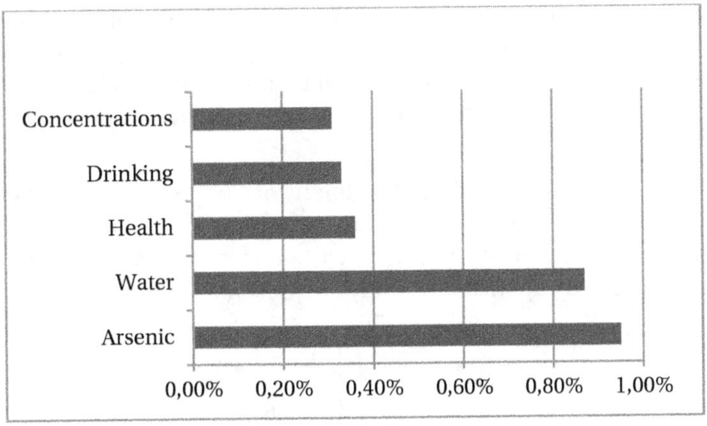

Chart 2. RAs written by students

A comparison of the five most frequently used words in both RAs written by experts and RAs written by novice writers point to the fact that novice writers tend to focus on the effects of arsenic on people's health more than on arsenic in general. Both charts indicate that *arsenic* and *water* are the two main words which are used in both specialized corpora. However, a deeper and more detailed analysis of the texts under scrutiny reveal other data which is worth our attention. When focusing on the articles written by experts, there are words such as *concentrations, samples* or *exposure*, which suggest that the medical geologists elaborating the RAs analyzed in this study address the topic of As in relation to its appearance in water and the levels of exposure people face when drinking the contaminated water. Conversely, the RAs written by students of Medicine present words such as *skin, cancer* or *lesions* which may indicate an interest in getting a deeper insight into the effects of As on people's health more than into As and its concentration in water and ground water. Admittedly, there are cases of words such as *cancer* in the RAs written by experts which also occupy a high rank in the articles analyzed, but the presence of health-related words in the articles by students is more salient.

Regarding the structure followed by the novice writers, results indicate that students followed the structure introduced during the lessons and as part of the seminar they attended on how to write a research paper. The structures followed in the two papers under study are presented below:

-Abstract	1. Abstract
1. Introduction	2. Introduction
1.1 Risk factors	3. Material and methods
1.2 Diseases	4. Results
1.3 Treatment	5. Discussion
1.4 Ongoing monitoring	6. Conclusion
2. Materials and methods	7. References
3. Discussion	
4. Conclusion	
5. References	

Tables 5 and 6 show the structures followed in the articles written by novice writers and which follow the structure taught in class. A comparison of the two structures suggests that, as seen in Table 5, the structure of article 1 is more elaborate than the one in article 2. For these authors, the abstract does not belong to the structure of the article *per se*, while article 2 shows how the abstract is fully incorporated as one of the essential parts of the article. Furthermore, article 1 elaborates on the introduction by subdividing it into four parts which address the theoretical background on As and its effects on human health. Conversely, article 2 does not present any subdivisions in the structure followed. These results, as was pointed out previously, point to the fact that the structure of article 1 is more elaborated and detailed than that in article 2. This suggests that the authors of article 2 may be more novice writers than those of article 1 and, hence, they still struggle with the handling of structuring and giving shape to research articles written in English.

Conclusions

This study was intended to prove the feasibility of the use of RAs written by experts for the teaching of English for Specific Purposes, in this case for the teaching of English for Medicine, with a special focus on MG as an incipient field of knowledge. The main interest lied on the use of RAs for the teaching and acquisition of technical words related to this field of knowledge and also for the teaching of writing skills by analyzing the structural patterns followed in RAs on this field of knowledge. In order to do so, two specialized corpora were compiled and a subsequent comparative analysis was carried out to study whether the use of RAs by experts', when compared to those written by novice writers had an effect on the writing skills developed by these novice writers who were asked to elaborate articles on As and its effect on human health.

Corpus-based techniques have proved fruitful and useful since it allows the analyst to work with real samples of language and to obtain reliable data on what can be found on RAs in MG. Furthermore, these data are used to work with students in the degree of Medicine, since these RAs have already proved useful in the teaching of oral skills in Medicine (see Diego, Pérez-Veneros and Elorza 2017). Learning of the English language, in this case, vocabulary, in a more relaxed environment has been confirmed following previous studies such as Pérez-Veneros (2016). The collected results shown and elaborated on in section 5 have shed light on how students have read, thought, researched and used key words in the field of GM with scientific vigor.

The implementation of focusing not on the language itself, but on "learning to think in the language" (Marsh 2000: 8) has been also determined on scientific jargon related to MG and which can be later on used by students on their own future research, whether it is to apply this vocabulary when writing research papers or when presenting their work to the scientific community in conferences and other scientific meetings. Comparative results observed in section 5 have illustrated the benefits of the approach in the syllabus design of an ESP course that, as surveys have confirmed, clearly helped the use of the academic structure during the academic year of 2017/2018.

The analysis of RAs through the use of corpus linguistics techniques in section 5 has been useful in teaching students how to write a research paper since the samples of language presented in the classroom are real (the RAs used have been written by experts in MG) so students can get a better idea of the layout of a RA and the main features which define its nature as well as the dissemination of MG as an emergent field of knowledge.

References

Primary sources

Research articles by experts in MG

Finkelman, R.B., Skinner, H. C. W., Plumlee, G. S., Bunnel, J.E. 2001. "Medical Geology." *Geotimes* 46(11): 20-23.

Giménez-Forcada, E., Vega-Alegre, M., Timón-Sánchez, S. 2017. "Characterization of Regional Cold-hydrothermal Inflows Enriched in Arsenic and Associated Trace-elements in the Southern Part of the Duero Basin (Spain), by Multivariate Statistical Analysis." *Science of the Total Environment* 593-594: 211-226.

Smith, A.H., Hira Smith, M.M. 2004. "Arsenic Drinking Water Regulations in Developing Countries with Extensive Exposure." *Toxicology* 198: 39-44.

Smith, A.H., Lingas, E.O., Rahman, M. 2000. "Contamination of Drinking Water by Arsenic in Bangladesh: A Public Health Emergency." *Bulletin of the World Health Organization* 78(9): 1093-1103.

Research articles by novice writers

Article 1: "Treatment of Chronic Arsenic Poisoning." Anonymous.

Article 2: "Health Effects Result in Exposure to Arsenic-contaminated Water, a Current Behavioural and Educational Research of the Population in Bangladesh." Anonymous.

Secondary sources

Anthony, L. 2014. AntConc (Version 3.4.4) [Computer Software]. Tokyo, Japan: Waseda University. Available at http://www.antlab.sci.waseda.ac.jp/ (Accessed on 24 Feb 2017)

Ball, P. and Kelly, K. 2015. *Oxford Handbooks for Language Teaching*. Oxford: Oxford University Press.

Bundschuh, J., PrakashMaity, J., Mushtaq, S., Vithanage, M., Seneweera, S., Schneider, J., Bhattacharya, P., Islam Khan, N., Hamawand, I., Guilherme, L.R.G., Reardon-Smith, K.; Parvez, F., Morales-Simfors, N., Ghaze, S., Pudmenzky, C., Kouadio, L., Chen, C.Y. 2016. "Medical Geology in the Framework of the Sustainable Development Goals." *Science of the Total Environment* 581-582: 87-104.

Centeno, J.A., Finkelman, R.B., Selinus, O. 2016. "Medical Geology: Impacts of the Natural Environment on Public Health." *Geosciences* 6: 8.

Coulthard, M. (ed.) 1994. *Advances in Written Text Analysis*. London: Routledge.

Coyle, D., Hood, Ph., Marsh, D. 2012. *CLIL. Content and Language Integrated Learning*. Cambridge: Cambridge University Press.

Diego Sánchez, J., Pérez-Veneros, M., Elorza, I. 2017. "Evaluating Course Implementation in Task-based Teaching: Students' Satisfaction of Oral Presentation Rubrics in an ESP Course." Paper presented at *41st AEDEAN Conference*. University of La Laguna (Spain), 8-10 November 2017.

Hyland, K. 2010. "Constructing Proximity: Relating to Readers in Popular and Professional Science." *Journal of English for Academic Purposes* 9: 116-127.

Fortanet-Gómez, I. 2013. *CLIL in Higher Education: Towards a Multilingual Language Policy*. Bristol: Multilingual Matters.

Hunston, S. 2013. "Systemic Functional Linguistics, Corpus Linguistics, and the Ideology of Science." *Text&Talk* 33(4-5): 617-640.

Marsh, D. 2000. "Using Languages to Learn and Learning to Use Languages: The Future doesn't just Happen, it is Shaped and Modelled by our Actions." In Marsh, D. and Langé, G. (eds.) *Using Languages to Learn and Learning to Use Languages*. Finland: University of Jyväskylä. 1-14.

Marsh, D., Pérez-Canado, M.L., Raez-Padilla, J. 2015. *CLIL IN ACTION: Voices from the Classroom*. Cambridge: Cambridge Scholars Publishing.

Muñoz, V.L. 2015. "The Vocabulary of Agriculture Semi-popularization Articles in English: A Corpus-based Study." *English for Specific Purposes* 39: 26-44.

Myers, G. 1990. *Writing Biology: Texts in the Social Construction of Scientific Knowledge*. Madison, WI: University of Wisconsin Press.

Myers, G. 1994. "Narratives of Science and Nature in Popularizing Molecular Genetics." In Coulthard, M. (ed.) *Advances in Written Text Analysis*. London: Routledge. 179-190.

Pecman, M. 2014. "Variation as a Cognitive Device: How Scientists Construct Knowledge through Term Formation." *Terminology* 20(1): 1-24.

Pérez-Veneros, M. 2016. "The British Press in High School: Potential Applications of the Popularization of Science in a Bilingual Educational Environment." Paper presented at *34th AESLA International Conference – "Professional and Academic Discourse: An Interdisciplinary Perspective"*. University of Alicante, 14-16 April 2016.

Sellinus, O., Allowa, B., Centeno, J.A., Finkelman, R.B., Fuge, R., Lindh, U., Smedley, P. (eds.) 2005. *Essentials of Medical Geology: Impacts of the Natural Environment on Public Health*. Burlington, MA: Elsevier Academic Press.

Smedley, P.L., Kinniburgh, D.G. 2002. "A Review of the Source, Behaviour and Distribution of Arsenic in Natural Waters." *Applied Geochemistry* 17: 517-568.

Spanish Ministry of Education. 2007. "Ley Orgánica 4/2007". https://www.boe.es/boe/dias/2007/04/13/pdfs/A16241-16260.pdf (Accessed on 18 January 2018).

Thomas, S., Hawes, T. 1997. *Theme in Academic and Media Discourse*. Monographs in Systemic Linguistics 8. Nottingham: University of Nottingham.

Thompson, P., Tribble, C. 2001. "Looking at Citations: Using Corpora in English for Academic Purposes." *Language Learning and Technology* 5(3): 91-105.

Tognini-Bonelli, E. 2001. *Corpus Linguistics at Work*. Amsterdam/Philadelphia: John Benjamins Publishing Company.

CHAPTER FOUR

Assessment Issues in ESP-Based College English Program Reform in China's Tertiary Educational Institutions: A Case Study Of CUFE

Shi Wenjie

Introduction

College English program in China

College English Program(CEP) in tertiary educational institutions in China was designed in the early 1980s by the Higher Education Department of the State Education Commission of China (renamed as the Ministry of Education of China in 1998) to embrace the reform and opening-up policy which will generate a rising demand for professionals with high command of foreign languages, particularly English. In accordance with the *College English Teaching Syllabus* (1985) that serves as a guideline for CEP, College English Courses will be delivered as required courses for bachelor degree programs at all tertiary educational institutions in China, which will be embedded into bachelor degree programs of all disciplines offered in tertiary educational institutions with a total credit of 16 points consecutively and evenly distributed in two academic years (*College English Teaching Syllabus* 1985 1986). *College English Curriculum Requirements* (2007) and *College English Teaching Guideline* (Pending Version 2015) are the updated guiding documents for College English Program in response to the changing scenarios of English language teaching in China.

College English Tests Band 4 and 6 (CET-4, 6) were developed and administered by the State Education Commission in 1988 to assess the undergraduates' proficiency & achievement attained from the CEP, and to ensure that students will have reached the levels prescribed by the *College English Teaching Syllabus* upon completion of the CEP. College English Tests are nationwide high stake test with formidable impacts for undergraduates: Failure in the

CET-4 by the time of graduation might disqualify the applicants' university bachelor degrees.

A huge number of ELT practitioners have looked at the effectiveness of CEP over the past decades in improving the students' language proficiency and communicative abilities in English (Cai 2011; Li 2016), and among them, some complained about the lower-than-expected efficiency of the CEP in improving practical communicative ability and that the overstated impact of CEP has undermined the importance of subject courses to some extent (Wang 2011; Zhang 2011). Meanwhile, there has been a widely accepted assumption that with CEP and CET implemented over the past three decades, the students in tertiary educational institutions have built up their language proficiency a noticeably higher level compared with that of 20 years ago. Consequently, as students' command of the language has been raised and learning needs were extended and diversified, the CEP is facing challenges and needs to be updated to tackle the blames from the students as well as the community as a whole.

Over the past decade, a new wave of College English Program reform has generated widespread concern, featured by Content-Based Instruction (CBI) and English for Specific Purpose (ESP) to meet extended and diversified learning needs and expectations from university students who are enrolled in top or key universities in China. Meanwhile, updated guidelines for CEP prescribe from educational authorities that the CEP should be localized at different colleges and universities in response to the individualized and diversified learning needs of students and the specific features of colleges and universities.

College English program reform in CUFE
Needs analysis of stakeholders

Hutchinson & Waters (1987, 19) argue that "ESP is an approach to language teaching in which all decisions as to content and method are based on the learner's reason for learning", and that ESP is a learning-centered approach to teaching which gives high priority to learners' needs in designing the courses. In order to figure out the learning needs more comprehensively, we adopted the needs framework by Hutchinson & Waters (1987) and divided the needs from three perspectives, namely the students' needs and wants, future employers' needs of language skills in the upcoming workplace, and academic needs of language skills from teachers in business and finance disciplines.

We applied questionnaires and structured interview to identify the needs of students, professionals and academic practitioners in the domain of business and finance. By aligning the findings from the data survey, we found that the top three specified focus of English courses in registers, genres, and skills are as follows:

1) Discipline-specific contents: the respondents expected the courses are business and finance specific;
2) Future occupation-related: they believe that the specific language used financial and commerce sectors are in need;
3) Language skills of communicative practice-based: the weakest skills for the respondents are speaking and writing skills in English. Therefore they expect the new courses give due importance to these two skills.

The findings also indicate that the interviewees expected the required courses to be shortened in terms of academic years involved, and they hoped the total credit attached to CEP to be reduced from the current total of 16 points. Because they believed that English courses were given too much priority over subject courses and more-than-needed time was wasted on them.

College English program redesign

According to Hutchinson & Waters (1987, 144) "ESP courses would equip particular learners with the necessary skills to carry out particular tasks in English". Following the needs analysis from the three stakeholders, we categorize the communicative language use tasks into specific academic and professional language use domains. Courses of English for Academic Purposes were designed by EAP team of teachers who have strong English literature academic background and intend to deliver EAP courses focusing on academic writing and presenting skills.

In addition, courses of English for Specific Purposes were designed with the syllabus focused on communicative skills for professional use in financial and commercial sectors. ESP courses will be undertaken by teachers with transdisciplinary academic experience or those teachers who demonstrate a strong interest in exploring ESP to enrich and transform their teaching. Finally, a new localized College English Program featured by multi-layered and multi-module courses specified for business and finance purposes in preparation for academic and professional use was constructed as in Figure 1.

Fig. 4.1: CEP of multi-layered and multi-module courses

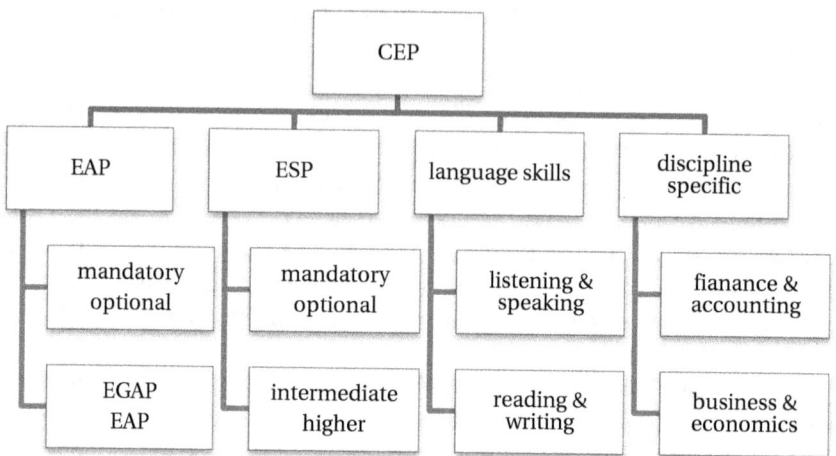

The ESP courses are multi-layered in that, first the EAP and ESP courses for business and finance are divided into varied levels in terms of the difficulty of the course content and language proficiency requirement for would-be applicants, where EAP is divided English for General Academic Purposes (EGAP) for intermediate level learners and EAP for higher level learners based on their performance in the placement test, and similarly, ESP is divided into intermediate and higher levels; and secondly the courses are categorized into mandatory and optional courses scheduled in the first three years of the four-year bachelor degree programs available for students registration. The new program is multi-module courses which contain speaking and writing modules in terms of language skills, and are composed of courses for academic and professional communication in multiple disciplines including economics, business, and cross-cultural studies.

With regard to the credit structure, the new CEP will have total credit for required language courses of 16 to 8 as a response to expectations from the survey on cutting total credit of required language courses and university-level credit restructuring for bachelor degree programs, meanwhile offering more optional courses in total of 8 to meet extended needs of those who want to keep learning languages following the required courses in language.

Outcomes of the new college English program

The follow-up investigation indicates that the satisfaction for ESP based courses is significantly higher than that of EGP courses for the same group of students who have experienced both the EGP courses and the ESP courses during the transitional period of the reform. The respondents believe that the

ESP courses enable them to be engaged in class activities of practical business or academic-related issues instead of non-specific ones in EGP classes.

However, the investigations conducted on students of different years of course taking (2014 vs 2015) reveal satisfactions have a minor dropping trend for the year of 2015 compared with that of 2014, which can be attributed to the follows:

1) the students' needs for courses are likely to be more diversified compared with prior respondents, but limited courses availability erodes satisfaction;
2) the students are likely to expect higher demands for instructors in terms course content and delivery, while course delivery might fail their expectations.

Therefore, steadily higher demands from the students are in a growing trend, which poses challenges to the new CEP as well as those teachers who involve themselves in the ESP-based college English program.

Reflections on challenges and opportunities

The new CEP creates opportunities from the following two aspects: 1) the diversified and multi-module courses are delivered to accommodate diversified and individualized needs of the students, which are expected to motivate the students in their language learning initiatives, and 2) the teachers inspired by the initiative to offer ESP-based courses instead of EGP courses in prior program are offered new direction in instruction. Therefore, the effectiveness of the new program generates research topics for in-class theoretical and practical studies.

The new CEP, however, exposes fresh issues of concern to teachers and school: 1) the sustainability of ESP-based & multi-module courses is challenged by limited human resources engaged in the reform project; 2) the diversity of courses poses new challenges for assessing courses from the perspective of teaching administration; 3) teacher career development and self-identification of their roles might be challenged as they are not sure to be labeled as language teachers or subject course teachers; 4) the assessment issues of the new ESP-based language courses need to be handled with care and focus, to assure the courses will achieve expected goals by properly designed ESP assessment framework.

Assessment issues in the ESP-based college English program

Course evaluation and learner assessment are assumed to be the areas of assessment in language instruction process, Hutchinson & Waters (1987) argue that course evaluation is to evaluate the degree to which the objectives being met, and to give feedback on future course design. Meanwhile, learner assessment is to test whether the learners have acquired the skills to fulfill the communicative task and to find out what has been learned and what the learner does not know about.

With regard to ESP assessment, the key issue is the same as language assessment, namely, what should be tested and how to test (Douglas 2013). Therefore, we will first analyze the construct of ESP assessment and how to conduct assessment by reviewing previous literature on the construct of ESP assessment, and then propose a procedure to assess the construct for EAP and ESP courses in the universities of finance and economics.

What is to be tested: the construct in ESP assessment

There remains a debate over the nature of the construct of ESP assessment since ESP research and assessment have been given more considerations since the 1990s by researchers (Douglas 2000; Elder 2001; Cheng 2010), who hold differing opinions on defining the construct of ESP assessment in contrast to that of language assessment for general purposes (Davies 2001; O'Sullivan 2006).

Davies (2001) believes that there is no difference between a general proficiency test and ESP test, language tests for either EGP or ESP are about abilities to use language functions properly in a huge variety of ways, from which we might assume that pure linguistic elements with varying degree of authenticity weigh over specific knowledge aspects.

Different from the focus on language core in ESP language assessment, Douglas (2000) argues that ESP test tasks allow for an interaction between the test taker's language ability and specific purpose content knowledge. In addition, Douglas (2013) reiterates the point by believing that the construct for ESP assessment includes linguistic knowledge and background knowledge in the communicative tasks, these two types of knowledge interact with each other with varying degree of authenticity, specificity, test context and precision, which make ESP assessment differed from EGP assessment. Barry O'Sullivan (2006) echoes the inextricable nature of subject knowledge in ESP assessment by arguing from the perspectives of business English that the construct of business English is explicitly definable, but linking test tasks with language needs to be worked on, believing that there a continuum of specificity between EGP and ESP assessment, by which EGP stands on one end and ESP falls on the other end.

The findings of Jacoby and MacNamara (1999) from Test of Medical English and evaluation of conference presentation practices arrive at the conclusion that sole linguistic elements excluding subject-specific knowledge in the construct of ESP assessment are insufficient to evaluate the performance in specific communicative tasks of medical domain.

We agree with the dispositions on the construct of ESP assessment by Douglas (2013) and Barry O'Sullivan (2006) on the grounds that the specified communicative tasks in ESP domain will not be fulfilled by solely manipulating language abilities or utilizing specific content knowledge. Therefore, ESP assessment differs from EGP assessment in that it not only assesses the linguistic aspects in the communicative task but also specified subject knowledge aspects involved in the task.

We adapt from the framework of construct for ESP assessment from Douglas (2013) and Barry O'Sullivan (2006), and arrive at the conclusion that the construct of ESP assessment should involve both language knowledge as well as specified subject knowledge used in the specific communicative tasks. In the ESP assessment domain of College English Program implemented in the Central Universities of Economics and Finance, we categorize the language abilities and specified subject knowledge for business and finance purposes into subcategories for EAP and ESP assessment illustrated in Figure 2.

Fig. 4.2: Breakdown of the construct of ESP assessment

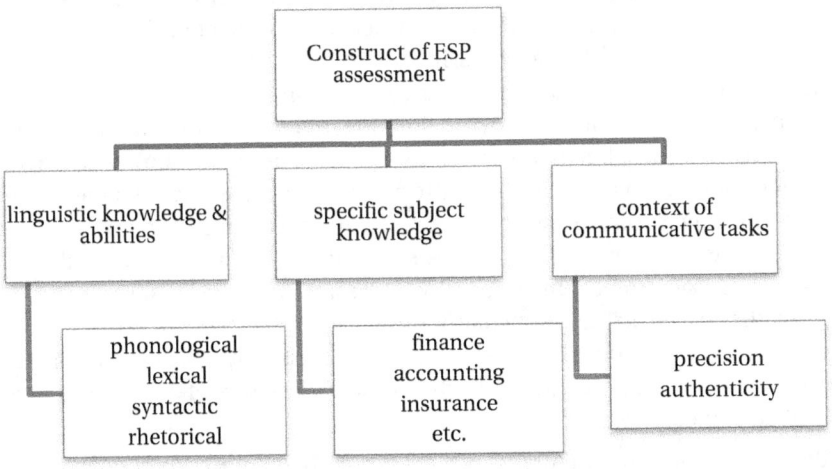

Linguistic knowledge and abilities contain phonological, lexical, syntactic and rhetorical knowledge demonstrated in the task, specified subject knowledge is composed of field-specific content, namely the degree of precision, authenticity related to the context in the domain of business and finance.

1) The construct for EAP assessment is focused on learners' linguistic knowledge and abilities, and the precision of subject knowledge related to the communicative task in the fields of academic study for business and economics in an international context;

2) The construct of ESP is focused on learners' linguistic knowledge and abilities, and the precision of subject knowledge used in the financial or business sector for professional purposes under international context.

How to test: the criteria and procedure

Having defined the construct for ESP assessment in CEP of Central University of Finance and Economics, we need to adopt the criteria of assessment from widely accepted language assessment criteria. Based on the purposes of the assessment in this study that are to examine the accurate achievement of the test takers over the courses, and to guide the students on ESP-based language acquisition, we give high importance to the standards of validity, reliability, interaction, impact, and practicality. Validity requires that the assessment of ESP courses balance the ratio of language knowledge and specified subject knowledge as to the construct definition and that the task types need to be as authentic as possible to the real communicative tasks. Reliability in this domain refers to the inter-rater and intra-rater consistency in the test results, and the score consistency between students who register the courses in varied academic years delivered by different teachers. Impact of the assessment will be easily noticed by teachers in the students' learning behaviors and learning strategies utilized during the course delivery and after the courses have completed. We aim to provide the students with enduring impacts on self-taught learning behaviors by devising the course syllabus focused on building motivation and learning patterns, and by designing the assessment procedure which contributes to integrated skills development in the specified communicative tasks. Authenticity is stressed on the grounds that the assessment is likely to be constrained by the test context and resources available for the test, which is particularly noticed in ESP assessment in that the simulated test situations in classes context can hardly meet the authentic business or academic context which requires expertise of assessors in the specified subject fields.

We devise a pattern of ESP assessment on the basis of the standards adopted in the assessment process as following chart in Figure 3

Fig. 4.3: Procedure of ESP assessment in CUFE

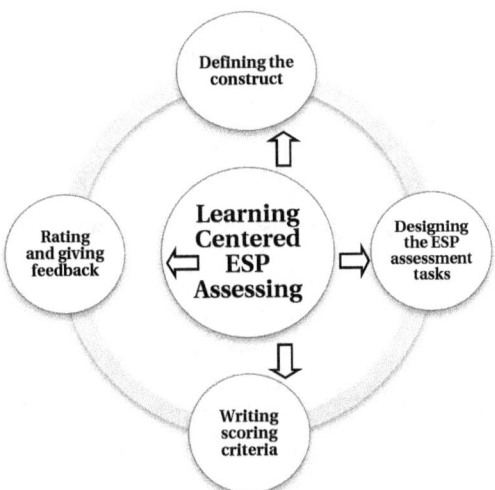

This assessment pattern is learning centered ESP assessing in that the four elements interactively serve the learning activities in a cyclical instead of linear way, where step 1 is defining the construct through investigating the specific target language use task; step 2 is designing the ESP assessment tasks by closely following the criteria of assessment; step 3 deals with writing scoring criteria and rubrics with reference to language abilities and content knowledge descriptors; and step 4 is about rating and giving feedback to students as well as course design.

This assessment pattern is a cyclical procedure with the factors mutually-affected and serving the learning-centered ESP assessment, whereby language teachers focus on language abilities and professional experts provide discipline-specific technical and knowledge support from the perspectives of specified subject knowledge.

The framework of ESP-based assessment in CUFE

Following the construct analysis and criteria description in the theoretical aspects, we touch upon the issue from practical perspectives by integrating formative assessment with summative ones, aligning speaking test with writing ones, balancing the ratios of receptive and productive items in the paper-and-pencil based final exam. The framework of assessment was designed as illustrated in Figure 4.

Fig. 4.4: Framework of ESP assessment in CUFE

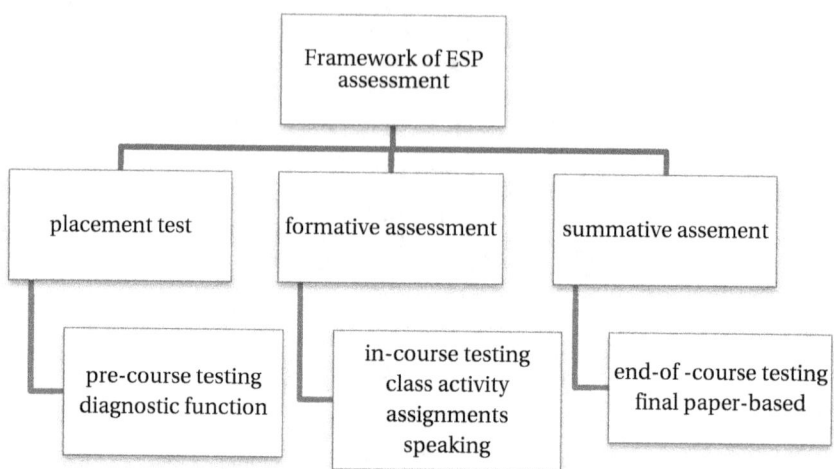

Placement test for diagnostic purposes will be conducted before the beginning of the CEP, which will help the students option for the ESP courses suitable for their current language proficiency. Each course will produce a final assessment report of the student achievement in the course in percentile format, which is formative and composed of following aspects: 1) attendance and participation (accounting for 20% of the final assessment); 2) writing assignments and speaking test (accounting for 20% of the final assessment); 3) speaking test by foreign teachers (accounting for 10% of the final assessment); 4) final written test (accounting for 50% of the final assessment). Students portfolio will be used to record the performance of the student in each sub test, which contributes to the final scores of those students.

This newly designed assessment framework for ESP courses differ from previous assessment framework as to test contents which will be involving both language abilities and specified subject knowledge, test structure which involves several sub-tests instead of only one paper-and-pencil-based final exam, and reliability guarantee of test results which will require inter-rater and inter-course agreement to secure the fairness of assessment by adopting both norm-referenced scoring and standard-referenced scoring.

Conclusion

There remains much debate over the issue of the construct of ESP assessment, on which much theoretical and practical exploration needs to be conducted in the context of English for business and finance purposes in the tertiary educational institutions in China, particularly, the expertise possessed by subject course teachers needs to be available for co-working on test design and administration.

There are more issues that might arise after we adopted the new CEP and the assessment framework, one prominent issue for ESP practitioners/teachers is the multiple roles imposed on them, including needs analysis based on target language use; syllabus writing for the courses of ESP; test tasks design for ESP assessment; rating for students' performance in a specified subject domain and the like.

"We recognize ourselves as someone between language instructors and subject course teacher, but we feel quite unconfident when delivering the business and finance related English courses", responded one teacher who began teaching English for accounting and finance in professional use with no prior academic engagement in business and economics. They are supposed to work hard by constantly updating subject knowledge and lifelong learning. However, we might be inspired by a quotation from the pioneers of ESP research like Hutchinson & Waters (1987, 163): "The ESP teacher should not become a teacher of the subject matter, but rather an interested student of the subject matter".

In addition, the current assessment framework remains subject to study from multiple perspectives as follows. Validity of the current assessment framework is likely to be undermined by ESP and EAP teachers who are mainly language professionals, and consequently, are inadequate in specific subject knowledge which is essential for assessment task design and rating; Inter-rate and intra-rater reliability are likely to be compromised by raters' variance in rating; Authenticity may not be secured by multiple factors: testing task, testing situation. Therefore, this project is still subject to evidence-based assessment validation

References

Cai, J. 2011. *A way out for EFL at Tertiary Level Education in Mainland China*, Shanghai: Shanghai Jiaotong University Press.

Dudley-Evans, T., St John, M. J. 1998. *Developments in English for specific purposes: A multi-disciplinary approach.* Cambridge: Cambridge University Press.

Douglas, D. 2000. *Assessing languages for specific purposes*, Cambridge: Cambridge University Press.

Douglas, D. 2001. "Language for specific purposes assessment criteria: where do they come from?" *Language Testing* 18, no. (2), 171–185.

Douglas, D. 2013. "ESP and assessment." In *The Handbook of English for Specific Purposes* edited by, Paltridge B. and Starfield S., 367-384. Chichester, UK: Wiley-Blackwell.

Davies, A. 2001. "The logic of testing languages for specific purposes." *Language Testing* 18, no. 2, 133 – 147.

Hutchinson T., Waters A. 1987. *English for Specific Purposes-A Learning-Centered Approach.* Cambridge: Cambridge University Press.

Jacoby, S., McNamara, T. 1999. "Locating competence." *English for Specific Purposes* 18, no. 3, 213 – 241.

Li, H. 2016. "On guideline for college English teaching and challenges for college English teachers." *English Language Teaching* no. 9, 77-87.

Ministry of Education of the People's Republic of China (the then State Educational Commission). 1985. *College English Teaching Syllabus (for students with Science major).* Beijing: The State Educational Commission.

Ministry of Education of the People's Republic of China (the then State Educational Commission). 1986. *College English Teaching Syllabus (for students with Arts major).* Beijing: The State Educational Commission.

Ministry of Education. 2007. *College English Curriculum Requirements.* Shanghai Foreign Language Education Press, Shanghai.

National College English Testing Committee. 2006. *CET-4 Test Syllabus and Sample Test Paper (Revised Version).* Shanghai: Shanghai Foreign Language Education Press.

National College English Teaching Advisory Board. 2015. *College English Teaching Guidelines (Version inviting suggestions).*

Wang, S., Wang, H. 2011. "An investigation into the current situation of College English teaching among colleges and Universities in China and its reform and developing directions." *Chinese Foreign Languages* 8, no. 5, 4-10.

Zhang, W. 2011. "Comparative Analysis of College English Syllabi -From the Ecological Perspective." *Modern Education Science* 8, no. 3, 149-150.

Central University of Finance and Economics, accessed Dec 1, 2017,

https://en.wikipedia.org/wiki/Central_University_of_Finance_and_Economics

CHAPTER FIVE

Improving Social Competences of Nursing Students in ESP Classes

Anna Stefanowicz-Kocoł, Monika Pociask

Introduction

Linguistic language learning activities in foreign language learning / teaching process are the core part of every classroom activity. The main aim of acquiring foreign language is to communicate, and communication is a complex and creative process. Using the language for communication requires not only the linguistic knowledge of certain aspects, language skills on the basis of phonological, lexical and syntactical elements but also mental, cognitive creativity. Language acquisition is a gradual process. Nobody is going to master it without practising step by step certain language activities. It can be compared to learning how to drive – first, you must turn the key, push in the clutch, select the first gear, press the gas and so on. It is the same with a foreign language. The first step is to acquire the skill of assigning sounds to letters and then recognise a group of sounds forming a meaning, associate words the learner hears with their meanings and so on. The last step is natural communication / meaningful interaction between speakers in the communicative act.

What are language learning activities?

Activity is an action or a set of actions undertaken by the learner to master or develop a skill, for example, a speaking activity is to develop the speaking skill. It is a conscious, cognitively demanding, practical, feasible, intended activity – the action of an individual the effect of which depends on stimulation, conducting, correcting and controlling that activity, as well as on the predictable basis of the oral utterance or written text (Woźniewicz 1976, 154 – 156). Each activity must obtain its aim, be done on the basis of an example given before its implementation, have clear instructions explaining how to implement it. Implementation (doing the task) is usually carried out under the supervision of the teacher, who decides about appropriate techniques for error correction, decides whether repetition is necessary (in case of a lot of mistakes), assesses the students' performance and gives feedback (Paliński 1987).

Categorization of language learning activities

The criteria for activities are types of language skills, elements of language, aspects of language use, the level of achieved communication, the level of acquired language competency and learning / teaching conditions. The activities could be aimed at practising one aspect of the language and one skill, for example, phonological awareness or speaking activity, or multiple aspects, multiple skill sets (blended skills). Following the criteria, activities could be divided into: productive activities (active learning activities) which develop productive skills: speaking, writing and non-productive ones (passive learning activities) which develop receptive skills: listening and reading; multi-task activities which develop more than one skill, more than one aspect or both; grammar and language based activities; introducing activities; pre-activities; communication based activities, reproductive activities; quasi-productive activities; follow-up activities; revising activities and testing activities; substitutional activities, transforming activities; simple, difficult, complicated; well-known by a learner, totally new ones (Figarski 2003, 142 – 146).

There are also specific types of language activities which are aimed at a particular way and style of learning. These exercises are to help to give the learners tips how to learn, which style is the best for an individual learner and so on. In the authors' opinion learning activities / tasks could be also categorized according to strategic learning preferred or used by a learner, self-regulation learning process (in other words the process in which the learners control their learning), context-specific actions of the learner (Rose 2012, 138), cognitive strategies, memory strategies (Rose 2012, 141), metacognitive strategies, compensatory strategies, affective strategies, social strategies, type of learners' intelligence, type of learning styles – global, analytic, auditory, visual, kinaesthetic (movement-oriented), tactile (touch-oriented) (Oxford 2003, 2 – 3), type of personalities (global, analytic, closure-oriented, open, thinking, feeling, extraverted, introverted learners) (Oxford 2003, 5 – 7).

Most linguists present the following classification of language activities: activities which are commonly called 'pre-linguistic' as they introduce certain necessary information before any communication may happen, communication based activities aimed at real communication with interaction in the communicative act, and quasi-communication activities which are like a bridge between 'pre-linguistic' and linguistic activities (Figarski 2003; Komorowska; 1988, Paliński 1987; Woźniewicz 1976).

The very first language exercises ('pre-linguistic ones / elementary ones) performed by a learner at the very beginning of language learning / teaching process are mostly drills (mechanical ones). Their aim is to introduce or repeat words, language chunks, common phrases or language structures, apply grammar rules and form correct language habits. They are repetitive, substitutive and transformative activities. They concern aspects of the language, for example, grammar, lexis or spelling. They could be changed into communication-based activities if communication aspect is applied to them. It happens when the aim of the activity overlaps a real-life situation in which the practised language aspect will be used. There must be a stimuli – willingness to get to know something (Komorowska 1988).

Communication-based activities are to practise communicative competency – the ability to use a language system in a real-life situation effectively, fluently and accurately (Komorowska 1988, 75). Such activities help to use the language autonomously by a learner in an authentic language communication act. However, the way to these activities leads through the quasi-communicative activities. They are based on lexical freedom without breaking sociolinguistic rules and require forming utterances which are analogical but not identical to the given ones (Pietrzyk 1995, 181).

Examples of pre-linguistic exercises include: repeating the same phrase "Nice to meet you" introducing a few times different interlocutors, forming simple sentences analogically to the given ones with the substitution of a new verb, changing the verbs from the simple present into the simple past. They acquire more communicative aspect if a real-life situation is shown in the instruction, for example, the learner is instructed to tell what he did yesterday after acquiring rules in the simple past and the ability to express themselves in the simple present. Actually, it is changing the verbs from the simple present into the simple past.

The performance of learning communication-based activities concerns for example: preparing scripts of dialogues, conducting dialogues, giving instructions, improvising drama or interview, making a written outline or summary of a nursing report.

Language activities for future nurses aimed at social competencies

Language learning activities for future nurses, as our study showed (Stefanowicz-Kocoł and Pociask 2017, 269; Sztejnberg and Jasiński 2013, 105 – 152, 193 – 227; Tengelin and Dahlborg-Lyckhage 2016, 3 – 9; Long 2016, 31 – 32), should concentrate mainly on speaking and listening exercises as an average nurse's main duty is to communicate and interact with the patient to meet their needs (Pociask 2007, 35 – 36, 48, 61). There is no appropriate nursing care without effective communication. What's effective communication? "Effective communication involves listening, engaging and responding with empathy, being honest and trustworthy, and doing what you say you will do.

It's also about eye contact, body language, tone of voice and attitude (...)" (Water and Whyte 2012, 16 – 18). To be effective while communicating means to be aware of, know how to implement and implement the so-called social competencies which are inseparably connected with effective communication. In general, a social competency is the ability to read the situation, take somebody's perspective and react appropriately to achieve successful communication preserving all ethical principles. If it is so, we – teachers are responsible not only for the language but also how it is used. In nursing students' ESP course books there are activities which concentrate on language and language aspects or language functions. Although these activities are concentrated on listening and speaking, usually not many and sometimes none are devoted to practising social competencies. The lack of such activities is visible and troublesome for nursing teachers who, like us, have observed not appropriate behaviours, verbal language as well as body language. That suggestion was also discussed and confirmed during the 3rd International ESP Conference and Summer School "Establishing the Predominant position of ESP within Adult ELT" which was held at the University of Niš (Serbia) from the 2nd to the 7th of July, 2017.

The authors of this article in the previous study described under the title "Improving Social Competencies of Nursing Students in ESP Classes" (2017) analysed the survey studying knowledge and experience concerning social competencies acquired during nursing studies. The outcomes clearly indicate that there is a significant need for continuing practising social skills, especially those in which cultural barriers, as well as ethical dilemmas, must be faced.

Examples of activities which have been chosen to be included in this article are directed mainly at student nurses whose level of English is described according to the Common European Framework of Reference for Languages as at least B1. The user of the language level B1 (in other words intermediate or 'threshold') "(...) understands the main points of clear standard input on familiar matters regularly encountered in work, school, leisure, etc., deals with most situations likely to arise while travelling in an area where the language is spoken, produces simple connected text on topics which are familiar or of personal interest, describes experiences, events, dreams, hopes and ambitions, and briefly give reasons and explanations for opinions and plans (...) (2001, 24)." Topics of these exercises were based on real-life events as the main aim of practising them is to find themselves as nurses in typical situations as well as new and unpredictable ones. The authors' main objective is to equip nurses with a tool to deal with change on a daily basis and still achieve effective communication featuring social competencies. We hope that the implementation of these exercises will be the first step to make students be more aware of social competencies and their importance in nursing care. The first two activities focus more on an operative knowledge of social skills (know-how). The next activities are more complicated as users have to interact, be engaged in a given situation, make a decision, think critically and face ethical dilemmas. Although as it was mentioned earlier most of the activities concentrate on spoken language (oral skills), reading activities are also involved as this skill helps in building vocabulary, expanding structures and prepares to self-directed learning through all life.

Examples of language learning activities on social competencies

Below there are some examples of activities which might be proposed for practising social competencies during English for Nurses classes. Each one concerns a problem which Polish students or nursing teachers have had to face. These problems have been chosen as the ones worth analysing in class to ensure nurses are better prepared for similar situations in real life.

The first two activities focus on practising everyday verbal behaviour in situations that do not need knowledge of specialised vocabulary but introduces the students to the problem of socially acceptable verbal interactions in a specific workplace such as nursing college or various types of healthcare institutions.

LANGUAGE LEARNING ACTIVITY 1

Decide if a person described in the given situation behaves politely or not. Explain why you think so. In case of an unacceptable way of behaviour, advise what a person should do to improve it.

1. You are a teacher giving a lecture to a group of students. Behind the door you can hear another group of students using offensive language. What do you do?
2. You are a teacher. You have observed that one student never greets you when meeting you but this student always says hello when you enter the classroom. How do you react?
3. You are a very elated and optimistic student. You can hardly stop smiling. Your teacher seems to be suspicious that you laugh at him. How do you behave?
4. Your general practitioner looks as if he were not satisfied with his job, but it is just your imagination. Later you see him taking a drug for a terrible headache. At the same time, you hear patients waiting outside the doctor's surgery calling him 'big headed, conceited, next to God'. What do you say?

LANGUAGE LEARNING ACTIVITY 2

Divide the given reactions into the acceptable and the unacceptable socially. Explain your choice.

1. In the outpatient clinic, an out-patient has come with a stool sample to give it to a nurse, but it is in the wrong container. The nurse explains it but at the same time looking at her colleague and showing her disgust. Next, the nurse gives the right container. The patient is to put the content from the old into new container in the presence of nurses and other patients. The nurse raises her voice and says: Please, do it in the bathroom!
2. A nurse in the surgery is waiting for two family members of a patient suffering from HCV virus type C. These family members are the patient's wife and son. They are to have blood test for detecting the possible presence of the virus. They are outside the surgery waiting for their turn together with other patients. The nurse speaks so loud about what is to be done and why that all patients hear it although the door is closed. Some patients move away from the woman and her son.

The following language learning activities pay attention not only to verbal behaviour but also to such aspects of communication as body language or tone of voice. Students are asked to consider various scenarios and evaluate the behaviour of the interlocutors. Later they also need to elaborate on that behaviour to ensure the patients are treated in the most appropriate way.

LANGUAGE LEARNING ACTIVITY 3

Watch a scenario and assess the tone of voice, body language, verbal language of the nurse as well as her behaviour towards the patient. Next form a similar dialogue between the nurses, between the nurse and the patient and between the nurse and the physician. While presenting your dialogues the rest of the students are to assess this time their classmates' tone of voice, body language, verbal language, etc.

https://www.youtube.com/watch?v=tHD4soSk5so

LANGUAGE LEARNING ACTIVITY 4

Watch some scenarios and decide what was appropriate and not appropriate. Explain why. If you don't like something, try to improve the situation.

https://www.youtube.com/watch?v=Dx4Ia-jatNQ

APPROPRIATE nursing care

NOT APPROPRIATE nursing care	HOW TO IMPROVE

Write down phrases and questions useful for your future work, for example: Where do these marks come from?

After discussing such situations in class future nurses become more aware of possible pitfalls and solutions. They also see that they need to keep an open mind to avoid prejudging a situation. Both misunderstanding and prejudging may harm the patient in many ways. Probably the most important issue is that lack of understanding patients' reactions, which may be caused by their lack of experience in dealing with social interactions in a foreign language, might lead to further negative consequences ranging from patients refusing treatment to nurses being accused of misdemeanour.

Conclusion

The process of learning how to behave in various social circumstances begins in families and the family is the main source of examples of behaviour which is needed to function successfully in any group. The basic social competencies are acquired mostly by observing and copying them. The first interactions a child has are those with its family members at home. While growing up the number of places where interactions take place and their various participants from our society increases. However, there are some situations which are specific to professional fields, and nursing is a perfect example of such a field. What seems to be taken for granted is that a professional nurse is experienced and equipped with verbal and non-verbal measures to function in healthcare institutions. Reality shows just the opposite. How many times have patients complained about not being understood rightly or misunderstood? How many times have they felt embarrassed although their interlocutor did not realize it?

On the one hand today's world offers easy access to information but on the other hand excessive amount of it actually deprives human beings of access to first-hand experience. As a result, living in a society is becoming more and more complicated, difficult to bear, although the term society assumes living together in harmony (Stefanowicz-Kocoł, Dordević 2017, 367 – 377). Unfortunately, real communication with adequate rules of behaviour, has been replaced with many various forms of communication offered by ever-changing technology, where socials code plays a less and less important role. Consequently, we cannot expect present-day student nurses to have the social competencies to function in healthcare institutions if they have not spent enough time considering people's behaviour and their possible reactions.

ESP teachers should feel responsible for their contribution to developing nursing students' competencies in foreign language classes. The first step is to make students aware of how significant social competencies are and why they need to be considered. The best way to do it seems to keep slipping social competencies into language activities. If it is possible to learn and teach social competencies the question arises: Do language learning activities regarding social competencies work and meet expectations? The answer to that question could be the subject of the next article.

References

Council of Europe, 2001. *Common European Framework of Reference for Languages: Learning, teaching, assessment.* Strasbourg: Cambridge University Press. Accessed May 11, 2017.
https://www.coe.int/t/dg4/linguistic/Source/Framework_EN.pdf.
Figarski, W. 2003. *Proces glottodydaktyczny w szkole.* Warszawa: Wydawnictwo Uniwersytetu Warszawskiego, 142 – 146.
Komorowska, H. 1988. *Ćwiczenia komunikacyjne w nauce języka obcego, wydanie pierwsze.* Warszawa: Wydawnictwo Szkolne i Pedagogiczne, 75.
Oxford, R. L. 2003. *Language Learning Styles and Strategies: An Overview.* GALA, 2 – 3, 5 – 7, accessed August 11, 2017.
http://web.ntpu.edu.tw/~language/workshop/read2.pdf.
Paliński, A. 1987. *Sprawność czytania w nauczaniu języka rosyjskiego, wydanie drugie.* Warszawa: Wydawnictwo Szkolne i Pedagogiczne.
Pietrzyk, I. 1995. "Realizacja tematyki dotyczącej prowadzenia i funkcjonowania biurowości w przedsiębiorstwach handlu zagranicznego na zajęciach z praktycznej nauki języka rosyjskiego." In *Tekst rosyjski w świetle innowacji językowych i socjokulturowych: materiały międzynarodowej konferencji naukowo-metodycznej (Warszawa, 18 – 19 maja 1995),* ed. Siergiej Chwatow. Olsztyn: Wydawnictwo ART, 181.
Pociask, M. 2007. *Nauczanie medycznego języka angielskiego na kierunkach pielęgniarskich w szkołach wyższych. PhD thesis under supervision of prof. Antoni Paliński.* Rzeszów: Uniwersytet Rzeszowski, 35 – 36, 48, 61.
Rose, H. 2012. "Language learning strategy research: Where do we go from here?" *Self-Access Learning Journal* 3, no.2, 138, 141, accessed August 11, 2017. https://sisaljournal.files.wordpress.com/2012/07/rose.pdf.

Stefanowicz-Kocoł A., Pociask, M. 2017. "Improving social competencies of nursing students in ESP classes." In *The Journal of Teaching English for Specific and Academic Purposes* 5, no. 2, 269.

Stefanowicz-Kocoł A., Dordević, D. 2017. "Intercultural Competency of ESP Students." In *The Journal of Teaching English for Specific and Academic Purposes* 5, no. 2, 367 – 377.

Sztejnberg, A., Tadeusz L. J. 2013. *Improving Nursing Practice. Education, Competencies, Communication, Quality/ Doskonalenie pracy pielęgniarskiej. Edukacja, kompetencje, komunikacja, jakość.* Płock: Wydawnictwo Naukowe NOVUM, 105 – 152, 193 – 227.

Tengelin, E., Dahlborg-Lyckhage, E. 2016. "Discourses with potential to disrupt traditional nursing education: Nursing teachers' talk about norm-critical competency." *Nursing Inquiry.* Accessed May 26, 20/17, doi: 10.1111/nin.12166.

Water, A., Whyte, A. 2012. "Communicating with compassion." *Nursing Standard* 26, no. 23, 16 – 18, assessed June 25, 2017. https://doi.org/10.7748/ns2012.02.26.23.16.p7488.

Woźniewicz, W. 1976. *Z zagadnień typologii ćwiczeń w kształtowaniu umiejętności mówienia w języku rosyjskim.* Rzeszów: Wydawnictwo Uczelniane Wyższej Szkoły Pedagogicznej, 154 – 156.

CHAPTER SIX

Cultural Sensitivity in Aviation English Communication

Vanya Katsarska

Linguistic and cultural diversity

Diversity has become a buzzword in the early 21st century. Diversity across countries and professional fields involves a range of variables such as gender, age, ethnicity, language, education, culture, etc. The exchange of employees from different backgrounds and nations has become the norm rather than the exception in the last two decades. Due to this eagerly embraced diversity and the fact that business, political, military, or social encounters occur between people from different lingua-cultural backgrounds, high competence in languages has become a priority for professionals all over the world. Effective international work cannot be achieved without effective language communication. According to the *Special Eurobarometer 386* report, 88% of Europeans think that knowing languages other than their mother tongue is very useful, and 98% of Europeans consider mastering other foreign languages as useful for the future of their children (2012, 7). Nowadays, the English language has turned into a lingua franca – it is the official language of organizations such as NATO, EU, OPEC, UN, World Bank, etc.; it is the working language at business negotiations, political summits, sports events; it has been accepted as the universal language of the air and the seas.

There are some fields where diversity, linguistic and cultural diversity, in particular, should not only be acknowledged but also harnessed and managed in the best way possible because otherwise it can endanger public safety and risk people's lives. Aviation is one of these fields. Eurocontrol states that about 26,000 civil aviation flights are handled daily by the European Air Traffic Management. These flights are operated by various airlines whose employees have different native languages and culture. This is why there are standards, rules, and regulations and they apply to aviation professionals all over the world. The mandated international language is English. In aviation, interpersonal skills are essential, and the ability to work with people from various linguistic and cultural backgrounds is the key to safety and success.

Security and defence is another field where linguistic and cultural diversity is a huge challenge. Nowadays, military operations are rather complicated, distinguished by ceaseless interactions between allies, enemies, and locals. Language proficiency and cultural awareness are key factors to accomplishing military tasks, whether it is establishing camps for refugees in Turkey, mediating conflicts in Africa or negotiating peace in Afghanistan. Multinational missions require collaborative planning and integrated command and control. The recent conflicts in the Middle East and the European migrant crisis reveal that leaders must be ready to work with a diverse set of national and international partners against a myriad of threats. Interoperability, which NATO defines as "the ability to act together coherently, effectively and efficiently to achieve Allied tactical, operational and strategic objectives", is of paramount importance and ensures the effectiveness of the military forces. Inadequate language proficiency, lack of awareness of the threats inherent in cross-cultural communications and language misunderstandings can crucially compromise the quality and safety of military missions. During military missions, communication is critical and unambiguous language exchanges can mean the difference between life and death.

The air force, a branch of a nation's armed forces, is traditionally responsible for aerial warfare. Recently, due to changes in the global security landscape, it has been steadily involved in operations other than war, such as peace support operations, counter-terrorism, humanitarian assistance, and disaster relief operations. International air-policing is another example of collective defence and solidarity. In order to be able to address both conventional and unconventional threats and remain sufficiently flexible in international missions, air force personnel need a common language and a cultural understanding of their partners.

English for Specific Purposes

Lingua-cultural diversity in the world has brought new perspectives to language teaching. English language training in European schools has acknowledged that diversity too and responded to the needs of the global world and of each particular profession. Researchers such as Hutchinson and Waters (1987), Dudley-Evans and St. John (1998) acclaimed the new field English for Specific Purposes (ESP) and outlined its basic characteristics. ESP is an approach to English language teaching that is driven by an analysis of what learners need to do in the language; it focuses primarily on the linguistic knowledge and skills required to undertake professional tasks and deals with topics and issues within a specific academic, professional or vocational field. It is goal-oriented language learning – learners study English because they must perform a task in their specialist subject in English. Content and methods in ESP are derived from an analysis of a specific purpose target language use situation so that they are authentically representative of content and tasks in the target situation. In the ESP courses, language is a means to achieve professional goals. The ESP courses are the starting point from which new educational opportunities arise, and a more integrated world is brought into being.

The main goal of professional communication is to transfer knowledge, skills, and experiences among experts. In case these experts are from different nationalities, English becomes one of the pre-requisites for a successful collaboration. Dan Douglas, in his book *Assessing Languages for Specific Purposes*, offers a framework of specific purpose language ability which includes the following components: grammatical knowledge (vocabulary, morphology, syntax), textual knowledge (how to structure and organize language), functional knowledge (ideational, manipulative, imaginative functions of language), and sociolinguistic knowledge (dialects, registers, cultural references) (2000, 35). Furthermore, another factor that determines effective multinational communication is culture. The cultural context influences language use and gives the words broader meanings. Success in international communication involves intertwining language knowledge with professional background knowledge and culture sensitivity. Efficient international communication cannot be accomplished merely by acquiring the syntax and semantics of English; often it is also necessary to adapt the language and behaviour according to the cultural mindset of the other person engaged in the professional communication.

English for military purposes courses and English for aviation purposes courses were developed in various higher education institutions all over Europe and became a part of their national strategies. The aviation English courses are further subdivided into English for pilots and air traffic controllers on the one hand and English for aircraft maintenance personnel on the other. These subfields have their specific lexical, semantic and syntactic language features, which allows specialists to communicate more precisely and accurately about aspects of their profession that outsiders sometimes find impenetrable. Fortunately, many of these European ESP departments have incorporated a specialized curriculum and syllabus and use tailor-made coursebooks and additional materials in aviation English. Unfortunately, at a great number of these departments, culture competence has often been underestimated due to the widespread belief that ESP is culture-free.

However, language and culture are inseparable – they are interconnected and influence and shape each other. This is true even for aviation English, which is standardized all over the world and adheres to prescribed sets of rules, regulations, and guidelines that apply to civilian and military professionals in all countries rather than to different practices based on individual languages and cultures. Besides, there is no culture-free language, and professional language is no exception. This is why teachers need to consider the culture element when teaching aviation English at a university level. They need to develop cultural awareness and integrate intercultural communicative sensitivity in the teaching of ESP, aviation English in particular. Thus, language teaching should always make some reference to culture.

It is not an easy task to define the concept of culture because it encompasses various elements – from religion to cuisine, from art to behaviour, from social habits to civilizations, from personal morals to national customs. Michael Byram narrows it down to the "shared beliefs, values and behaviours of a social group" (2003, 50). Following this train of thought, we could say that culture represents a set of common values, beliefs, concepts, principles, and a way of life that is shared among individuals in one entity. Actually, culture is not limited only to a nation, with its associated heritage, customs, and traditions. Culture is also present in a community, social group, organization or profession, and it is manifested as one common pattern of behaviour and/or way of thinking distinguishing the members of one entity and another.

Cultural diversity is as multi-faceted as communication itself. Culture encompasses various interrelated layers and they can be explicitly expressed or implicitly embodied in the language. For instance, one of the challenges for a cadet pilot or aeronautical engineer in Bulgaria could be the different units of measure. In aviation, both metric (SI) and customary (imperial) units continue to coexist. Feet, metres, statute miles, nautical miles, inches of mercury, millibars, hectopascals, knots, metres/second – many people find this a bit disconcerting. Bulgaria uses the metric system. The USA uses predominantly the customary system. After the accession of Bulgaria to NATO, pilots and other personnel have become regularly engaged in US or NATO training, military exercises and multinational air force events. Sometimes it is not an easy task to adapt the language. In the USA, pressure is reported in inches of mercury measurement. Hectopascals dominate the rest of the aviation world, including Bulgaria. The altimeters in Western aircraft are calibrated in feet. When an air traffic controller clears a pilot to descend to 3600 metres, they should descend to the equivalent of 11,800 feet. Although in aviation global standards are being set, teachers should still draw students' attention to possible differences in the measurement systems.

Civil aviation has suffered due to the incorrect use of measurements. The case of Air Canada flight 143 in 1983 for example: a Boeing 767 flying from Montreal to Edmonton via Ottawa ran out of fuel about an hour into its flight. The problem was partially due to a human error – the maintenance workers did not take into account the difference between pounds and kilos; they communicated to the ground crew only a number. As a result, the aircraft ended up with less than half of the required amount of fuel on board, which threatened the lives of passengers and crew.

Hofstede's cultural dimensions theory dimensions

As English is the lingua franca, the ESP learner should build a culture awareness not only of the culture of the native speakers of English but also of the individual members they communicate within their profession, organization or community. ESP is the global language; so is the culture. However, building culture awareness in an English class is a challenging task. Cultural competence is a process that develops gradually over an extended period of time. Fortunately, there are empirically proven analytical tools to understand culture and prevent potentially dangerous miscommunication. A tool at the disposal of ESP specialists is the cultural dimensions theory of Geert Hofstede, a Dutch professor in psychology, and his followers, Canadian psychologist Michael Harris Bond and the Bulgarian scholar Michael Minkov. It discusses the three facets of culture: the culture of a nation and a society, the culture of an organization and the culture of a profession. The three cultures shape one's actions, attitudes, and language. These three facets of culture play their roles in aviation – a high-risk multi-cultural environment that requires excellent coordination among members. The culture of a nation, with its set of common values, concepts and beliefs, and of a society, with its knowledge, patterns of behaviour and practices, are deep-seated in the human mind and in most cases, they are highly resistant to change. This means most representatives of a given national culture have common personality characteristics that stand out when they meet with representatives of other nations. The culture of an organization and the culture of a profession are more flexible and can be modified if there are strong incentives. All three cultures are of importance in aviation because they may have an impact on language critical behaviours. These include how subordinates relate to superiors; juniors treat seniors and what words and expressions are used to share information. Culture may influence attitudes about stress, personal capabilities and adherence to standard operating procedures. Each of the three cultures has its strengths and weaknesses. The strengths enhance safety and the weaknesses diminish it.

National culture as explained by the cultural dimensions theory and its relationship to aviation

In the cultural dimensions theory, the power distance index (PDI) is the first dimension of national culture. The PDI is connected by the hierarchical order in a society and the equality among members of a nation and of a community. It expresses the degree to which people accept that power is not distributed equally. Nations that have high PDI are the ones with powerful leaders and a strict hierarchy, where everybody has their place and does not question it. Air force personnel, being part of the military, show a moderately high power distance culture, which might influence their language. In the air force, superiors use mostly direct and instructional language while subordinates volunteer information, suggest solutions to problems and question the actions of a superior only if it is really necessary. Thus, the PDI may have a negative impact on aviation safety. Robert Helmreich, a scholar of aviation psychology, states that in cultures of high power distance, a first officer should be trained that correcting or questioning the captain is not a sign of disrespecting the captain or being rude to them but more about safety and preventing incidents or accidents (1999:39-43).

Individualism versus collectivism dimension. This dimension is about identity and relationships with others. It determines if the goals and aims are individually oriented or team oriented. The cultures of countries like the USA or many countries in Europe value direct communication, independence, and self-sufficiency. People express their own opinions and try to resolve conflicts rather than simply agree. As a result, language is explicit, unambiguous and objective. Whereas in collectivist cultures, people value the team and they work to fulfil their obligations to it. The language is more elaborate, often ambiguous and in accordance with the group harmony. In the cockpit or operating theatre, this dimension may determine what language is used during the decision-making process and the resolving of conflicts.

Masculinity versus femininity dimension. Societies with a masculine-oriented culture value competitiveness, achievements and financial success whereas societies with a feminine-oriented culture, such as the Scandinavian countries, prefer cooperation, social benefits, modesty, and care for the quality of life. In general, all nations try to balance these two sides of the dimension. The masculinity side of this dimension is typical of military organizations. If there are no established rules, cooperation with other masculine cultures is challenging. It can lead to unjustified conflicts if partners try to dominate each other. However, the lack of decisiveness and competitiveness in the feminine-oriented culture may be interpreted as weakness by the masculine cultures. Thus, adjusting messages and actions to account for this dimension can lead to more effective intercultural communications.

The uncertainty avoidance dimension. This dimension is connected with dealing with unpredictability. It relates to rules and order. The high side of this dimension expresses the degree to which members need procedures and strict time limits for all situations and activities. Members assume that rules must not be broken, even if there is a possibility of the safety or interests of the organization being jeopardized. On the one hand, aviation respects and requires regulations so in all routine situations the aviation personnel of nations with a high degree of this dimension are doing an excellent job and there are no glitches. However, on the other hand, in non-routine situations, those nations with a low side of this dimension may be more effective at finding ways to cope with critical situations.

Normative versus pragmatic. This dimension is connected with the societal orientation to the present and the future. Nations with a more pragmatic approach focus on thrift, perseverance, and efforts in education to prepare for the future. Nations with a low degree in this dimension value traditions and look at changes in society with suspicion. In the cockpit, this dimension may influence the pilot's and co-pilot's behaviour if they try to yield to the need to prevent conflict or save face. In such a situation, instead of direct error negotiation, some people may try to let it pass unnoticed or avoid the confusion by not mentioning it. For example, the plane crash in Guam of Korean Air in 1997 was partly due to the hierarchical culture in Korea. During the flight, there were some problems and adverse weather. The pilot made an error, and the co-pilot did not correct him because he treated his commander with great deference. As a result, the airplane flew into a hill, and 228 out of 254 people died.

Indulgence versus restraint. This cultural dimension explains the degree to which people try to control their desires based on the way they were brought up. Nations with a high degree of indulgence focus on individual joy and well-being, on happiness and quality leisure time, on freedom of speech and personal control. Employees in these nations are more likely to leave their work position if they are not satisfied and happy there. On the other hand, restraint stands for a society that regulates and curbs these characteristics by means of strict social norms. Employees of these nations are not as willing to voice their personal opinions and share feedback.

An understanding of cross-cultural differences and similarities is important. Language and cultural barriers may lead to miscommunication. For instance, the scheduled Avianca Flight 052 from Bogota, Colombia to New York on 25 January 1990, is a tragic example of how cultural legacy can contribute to a disaster. In addition to weather and fuel miscalculations, investigators blamed the crash that led to the death of 8 crew members and 65 passengers on the crew members' proficiency in English and their culture. According to Hofstede's scale, Colombia has a high PDI, and it is a masculine and collectivist country. Before the missed-approach procedure, the first officer said to the air traffic controller (ATC): "We're running out of fuel, sir" when he should have declared an emergency due to a shortage of fuel. After the missed approach, the ATC told Avianca 052 that he was going to "...bring you about 15 miles northeast and then turn you back for the approach. Is that fine for you and your fuel?" The first officer replied, "I guess so, thank you very much." Actually, instead of this reply, he should have asked for a priority landing. The first officer was too deferential, too soft and respectful to the ATC because he considered him superior. Due to his culture, he was reluctant to object to the ATC's suggestion for a new route. His cultural background influenced his English and he never explicitly informed the ATC of their emergency situation.

Professional culture as explained by the cultural dimensions theory and its relationship to aviation

Another facet of culture is the professional culture associated with being a member of a profession. Pilots, businessmen, doctors, journalists, etc. share an occupation, and their professional culture becomes a common bond. It is very often formed around the values, beliefs, and traditions of the senior members and they pass this culture to the recruits.

Positive aspects of the culture of pilots are their self-confidence and pride in their profession. Their intrinsic motivation and dignity help organisations work toward safety and efficiency in operations. However, the professional culture of pilots can also be a peril. Most pilots consider themselves smart, sharp, quick, and invulnerable. They believe that their decision-making is as good in an emergency as in a routine situation, that their performance is not affected by feelings, and that they do not make more job errors in situations of high stress or personal problems.

Soldiers, on the other hand, inherit loyalty, discipline, and responsibility from their predecessors and their professional lives are distinguished by high moral standards. This is why valour is the invisible trait of all military pilots (Mihov 2017, 178). Military officers are the epitome of patriotism and self-sacrifice for their country.

Organizational culture as explained by the cultural dimensions theory and its relationship to aviation

The final facet is organizational culture. Each organisation has its own culture that is closest to the daily activities of their members. Professor Hofstede defines culture as "the collective programming of the mind distinguishing the members of one organization from another" (2010, 6). In this short definition, he emphasizes the importance of belonging. Individuals in one organization share values, knowledge and traditions. The purpose of sharing these patterns of values and beliefs in organisation culture is to provide, as Stanley Davis emphasizes, the members with the rules of behaviour of the organisation (1984, 29).

Organizational culture can differ even among organizations operating in the same country. For example, the air force has a rigid hierarchical structure and it does not tolerate any deviations from the regulations and the standard operating procedures. In most cases the language is more direct and authoritative, instructions are not blurred by polite expressions and orders are explicit. Whereas the civilian airlines have a company structure where people treat others as more or less equals and they are slightly more tolerant of deviations. There is greater mitigation in language communication and some instructions are softened by the use of modal verbs such as "would you…" or "could you…" Although both organizations belong to the field of aviation, behaviour and language among personnel can sometimes differ because of the organizational culture differences.

Since the 1990s human factor researchers such as Wiegmann and Shappell (2003) have started analysing aviation accidents deeper and have found that not the pilot as an individual but pilots as members of organizations and their culture were the cause of many accidents. James Reason calls these accidents "orgax", i.e., organizational accidents (1997, 2), and describes foresight training – measures that should make people aware of the situational risks (2016, 87). This paradigm shift was the result of the new interpretation of safety as a system and consideration of the multiple causes of accidents which interacted with each other.

A survey, which aimed to elucidate some aspects of the professional and organizational culture of Bulgarian air force personnel, was conducted in 2016. The questionnaire was given to 30 active duty officers, who work as fighter pilots and helicopter pilots in Bulgarian military bases, and 12 cadets-military pilots studying at the aviation faculty, National Military University, Bulgaria. The officers were between the ages of 29-36, with 29 males and 1 female, while the cadets were between the ages of 19-21, with 8 males and 4 females. All the participants knew the purpose of the questionnaire in advance and were assured of the confidentiality of their responses. Military people, including pilots, spend a significant amount of time together at work and they establish strong interpersonal bonds as well as a strong organizational/professional identity. The questionnaire revealed the following: 100% are committed to their profession, they have always dreamed of being pilots, they are proud of their profession and 72% are morally committed to their organization; they accept the organization's goals as their own personal goals and identify themselves with the long-term goals of the organization. They continue employment with their military organization because they want to do so and indicate a desire to continue their membership in the organization. However, the other 28% are committed to their profession, but they are not so much committed to their organization. They would prefer to change it for a civilian airline company. Most of these aviators admit they are unable to leave the military because they have governmental contracts while a very small percentage say they stay because they can see no viable alternatives to their current circumstances. This 28% are dissatisfied with their jobs because promotions and pay raises are usually slow in coming and based on seniority. The other 72% would disregard some disadvantages in their conditions because their flights are intensive, involving complex manoeuvres or stunts, and they earn a steady income. It might be worth noting that this number can fluctuate a lot depending on external factors such as the overall standard of life and the current economic situation of the military personnel in Bulgaria. An examination of organizational commitment over time might yield very different results.

Conclusion

Cultural differences, national, professional or organizational, influence language use. ESP teachers, aviation English teachers in particular, should revisit their understanding of efficient ESP teaching and focus their attention on building knowledgeable graduates with practical skills and competences. In aviation language teaching, these competencies consist of specific linguistic competence, which is pertinently determined for workplace needs; background competence, which is necessary to qualify graduates as members of their particular aviation profession; and cultural competence, which contributes to a successful and efficient communication. In relation to cultural competences, it should be noted that the role of the ESP teacher is not to make students accept a particular culture or behave in accordance with its conventions. The ESP teacher should only make them aware of the existence of various cultures and the relationship between culture and language. In a nutshell, efficient ESP teaching requires curriculum designers and teachers to go beyond the traditional ways of teaching English, which emphasizes only language knowledge and skills and introduces a triple bottom line: language skills, background knowledge, and cultural sensitivity.

Acronyms

ATC – Air traffic controller

ESP – English for Specific Purposes

ICAO – International Civil Aviation Organisation

NATO – North Atlantic Treaty Organization

PDI - Power distance index

References

Avianca Flight. Retrieved from: http://www.nytimes.com/1990/02/05/nyregion/avianca-flight-52-the-delays-that-ended-in-disaster.html?pagewanted=all

Byram, M., Grundy, P. 2003. *Context and Culture in Language Teaching and Learning*, Multilingual Matters.

Davis, S. 1984. *Managing Corporate Culture*, Ballinger.

Douglas, D. 2000. *Assessing Languages for Specific Purposes.* CUP.

Dudley-Evans, T., St. John, M. J. 1984. *Developments in English for Specific Purposes.* CUP.

Helmreich, R.L. 1998. *Building Safety on the Three Cultures in Aviation.* In Proceedings of the IATA Human Factors Seminar. Bangkok, Thailand.

Hofstede, G., Hofstede, G. J., Minkov, M. 2010. *Cultures and Organizations: Software of the Mind.* Revised and Expanded 3rd Edition. New York: McGraw-Hill USA.

Hutchinson, T., Waters, A. 2017. *English for Specific Purposes: A learning-centred approach.* CUP, 1987.

Mihov et al. *Порталът към небето и звездите*, Air Group 2000.

NATO. Retrieved from: https://www.nato.int/cps/ic/natohq/topics_69269.htm?selectedLocale=en

Reason, J. 1997. *Managing the Risks of Organizational Accidents.* Ashgate Publishing Limited.

Reason, J. 2016. *Organizational Accidents Revisited.* CRC Press.

Special Eurobarometer 386. 2012. *Europeans and Their Languages Report.* Retrieved from: http://ec.europa.eu/commfrontoffice/publicopinion/archives/ebs/ebs_386_en.pdf.

Wiegmann, D. A., Shappell, S. A. 2003. *A Human Error Approach to Aviation Accident Analysis: The Human Factors Analysis and Classification System.* Burlington, VT: Ashgate.

CHAPTER SEVEN

The Use of Lexical Bundles in Korean Learner Corpus – Directions for ESP Pedagogy

Jungyeon Koo

Introduction

English is a global language. Given its status as lingua franca (Hoffman 2000), there is a far-reaching need for fluent English speaking and writing in all sectors of life, particularly in academia, where conventionalized high-proficiency English is required. As the nativeness of non-native writers has become increasingly important, a multitude of studies have explored the elements of well-written prose and how best to teach them to English learners in academic contexts (Salazar 2011). A central one of these elements in the academic context is the use of frequently recurring word combinations that have been regarded as markers of language proficiency and of a particular register associated with academic writing (Cortes 2004).

The study of recurrent word combinations has been adopted in various forms by different scholars. Some focus on clusters (Hyland 2008a), recurrent word combinations (Altenberg 1998; Lindquist 2009), n-grams (Stubbs 2007), or lexical bundles (Biber & Barbieri 2007). These terms indicate continuous word strings retrieved by taking a corpus-driven approach with specified frequency and distributions criteria. The retrieved recurrent sequences are fixed multi-word units with conventional pragmatic and/or discourse functions employed and recognized by the speakers of a language within certain contexts (Chen & Baker 2010). What is interesting is a corpus-based study of language use has increased since 1999, such as Biber et al., (1999), Cortes (2004, 2006), Hyland (2008a, 2008b) and Simpson & Ellis (2010). These studies provided insights into the functional significance of highly frequent recurrent sequences of words, especially LBs in various disciplines. Throughout this study, Lexical Bundles (LBs) is adopted as the primary term to refer to recurrent word sequences that occur in academic register, as has been used by

Biber in his series of studies on which is based the theoretical framework of this study.

Literature Review

Previous Studies of Lexical Bundles

Certain Lexical Bundles (LBs) have been considered markers of proficient language use in a particular register, such as in academic writing (McCulley 1985). Most previous studies adopt the framework by Altenberg (1998) and Biber, Johanesson, Leech, Conrad, and Finegan (1999) in their seminal studies that found frequency-based recurrent word sequences and analyzed them based on grammatical structures and discourse functions.

For structure classification, bundles have commonly been classified into noun phrase (NP)-based, prepositional phrase (PP)-based and verb phrase (VP)-based bundles with each having multiple subcategories.

For discourse functions, most of the previous studies of written data classified their lexical bundles into three major categories. Referential bundles are those expressions making reference to entities or describing their attributes. They have three sub-categories, i.e., identification, specification of attributes who are subdivided into quantity and intangible framing, and deitic expressions (time, place, text reference). Secondly, stance bundles express the writer's knowledge of or attitude toward the proposition that follows or assessment of its certainty. They can be subdivided into epistemic, attitude or modality stance, which have their sub-categories (desire, obligation, intention/prediction, and ability). Lastly, discourse organizers are used to define relationships with preceding or following discourse in text performing specific functions such as topic introduction or focus and topic elaboration or clarification. It should be noted, however, that some categories of discourse functions and their subcategories used in these studies have not been clearly defined inviting much arbitrariness or subjectivity in classification (Ädel & Erman 2012).

The study on LBs has devoted attention to many researchers. In a series of scholarly works (Biber &Barbieri 2007; Biber, Conrad & Cortes 2004; Biber 2006), they observed that conversation and academic prose display different uses of LBs. Cortes (2004) explored the difference in the use of LBs in academic prose by published authors and by students at three different proficiency levels. If the subjects did employ LBs, they did so in different ways. In particular, Coates found that LBs were highly frequent in professional writers' corpora, but LBs were rarely published used in natives students' writings. This study showed LBs are not naturally acquired although native students' writers are graduate ones. She emphasized not only the exposure to the use of LBs in reading materials in formal instruction to the students in terms of the frequency and function of LBs in different disciplines.

Hyland (2008b) examined the structures and functions of research articles, doctoral dissertations, and Master's theses in four disciplines. He observed that there was disciplinary variation in the use of LBs across the four fields. Hyland (2008a) also conducted a similar study on published academic prose and postgraduate writing. He found that postgraduate students are more likely to adapt formulaic expressions than native scholars.

Chen & Baker (2010) followed the same line of research and investigated different uses of LBs in academic writing. They investigated LB uses among three groups: published authors, native student writers, and non-native writers. A wider range of LB use was found in writings of published authors than that of students, and the two student author groups displayed some distinctive uses of their own.

Ädel & Erman (2012) expanded the scope of their research to the structures and functions of LBs. They examined and compared LB use in writings of native speakers and advanced learners. They found that both a larger number and a greater variety of LBs were used by native speakers, findings that resembled the phraseological research tradition in Second Language Acquisition.

Lee (2012) explored the use of LBs in academic writing by native and non-native speakers. The author observed that non-native writers demonstrated the overuse of certain expressions and the underuse of others, as well as some structural differences. Similarly, Salazar (2011) in his doctoral dissertation identified specific LBs that non-native scholars overuse, which involves unnecessary repetition, lack of variation, and a limited use of participant-oriented bundles.

As shown above, most previous studies on LBs in the academic register have primarily emphasized the fields of linguistics and life sciences. Linguistics has been selected due to the texts' availability to the researchers. Life sciences are selected for study because of the difficulty faced by many non-native scientists and the high possibility for application of the research.

In this regard, Yang (2017) first examined LB use in a different genre of academic writings: narrative writings and argumentative writings written by Chinese EFL university students retrieved by kfNgram. His study classified LBs in terms of structural and functional categories based on Biber et al.'s (1999) taxonomy. The findings indicate that the students employed more four-word bundles in argumentative writings than in narrative compositions. Interestingly, there was no great difference between the two types of writings in their structural patterns. The study also found that the students used stance bundles more than the other functional types of bundles in argumentative writings, and they employed referential expressions other than stances bundles or discourse organizers in narrative compositions.

The next section will provide an overview of previous literature studies on LB use by Korean EFL learners.

Lexical bundles from Korean Learner Corpus and the purpose of the study

Choi (2015) conducted a corpus-driven study on frequency, structure, and function of LBs in linguistic research articles written by native speakers (NSs) of English and non-native speakers (NNSs) of English. She found that NNSs used LBs more frequently than NSs did but with less variation, primarily relying on common metadiscursive bundles. The two groups showed similar proportions of structural frequencies in LB uses: Prepositional Phrase (PP)-based used at the highest frequency, then Verb Phrase (VP)-based, then Noun Phrase (NP)-based. Functionally, the NS and the NNS groups also displayed a similar pattern of favoring categories of LBs: first, text-oriented, then research-oriented, then participant-oriented. However, the patterns within those categories were different: the NNS scholars preferred the first personal pronoun *I/we* while the NS favored indirect patterns such as anticipatory-*it* structures. In addition, the NNS scholars showed a varied use of hedges, which runs contrary to the previous literature. The findings indicate that the diversity in the various uses of native bundles indicated the NNS scholars' "expertise," while NNSs' extensive usages of modal and speech-act verbs displayed their "non-nativeness".

Lee (2009) and Kwon & Lee (2014) observed LBs from a spoken corpus of teaching demonstrations by Korean university students' and Korean EFL teachers' spoken data, respectively. These two studies found, by comparing and contrasting against corresponding spoken corpora of native speakers, that Korean learners overused limited sets of bundles that were mostly clausal in structure and functional in stance.

In contrast, Kim (2013) and Hong (2013, 2015) found, by comparing LBs from a corpus of Korean university students' English argumentative writing with those from a corresponding NS-student corpus, that the Korean student writers displayed overuse of the "personal pronoun plus verb" construction to express their stance (e.g., *I think it is, I do not agree*) and underuse of NP and PP-based LBs.

The above studies are of limited usefulness in suggesting any pattern of LB use in argumentative writings by Korean EFL students. Kim's (2013) study conducted research with a corpus of limited size, so it might not show a sufficient range of bundles used by Korean EFL students. Hong's (2013, 2015) studies used a larger corpus, comparable to the reference corpora employed in this study, but appeared to lack clear criteria in identifying and classifying bundles.

Yoon & Choi (2015) examined four-word LBs from a corpus of argumentative essays by Korean university students and compared them to bundles from a corpus of NS students' uses in argumentative writings. They found that the Korean university students evinced an over-reliance on bundles widely used in speech registers, such as contacting personal pronouns and contraction forms and on expressing stance in terms of grammatical structures and discourse functions. However, the Korean student writers displayed fewer uses of nominalization, hedging, and referential bundles due to the register feature (argumentative writings) and the lack of register awareness.

According to the previous literature, a smaller NNS corpus was used compared to the reference data (NS corpus), and some classification of LBs was unclear or unrigorous. Moreover, the research was primarily focused on NNS and NS scholars' articles. To correct for this, the current study chooses a larger selection of student data, YELC (Yonsei English Learner Corpus), which is a collection of 3,286 argumentative writings by university students, and compares that to a reference corpus, LOCNESS (Louvain Corpus of Native English Essays).

Therefore, this study purposes to address the following three research questions:

1) Compared to the usage of LBs by NSs (LONCNESS), what is structurally distinct about that of NNSs (YELC)? What are the commonalities and differences between the two groups of writings in terms of structural classifications?
2) Compared to the usage of LBs by NSs (LONCNESS), what are the functional traits of that of NNSs (YELC)? What are the commonalities and differences between the two groups of writings in terms of functional classifications?
3) How are the findings different or similar from the previous literature? Does the current study suggest pedagogical implications for how to teach students LB usage in academic prose in Korean EFL context? What are the implications in ESP teaching?

Data and analysis

Data

LBs are not simple expression and they have been shown to be rarely used by students (Coates, 2004). In addition, LBs are very frequently employed in published scholars' academic writing are disciplined-bound (Coates, Jones & Steller, 2002).

The data used in the study was drawn from a Korean learner corpus, the Yonsei English Learner Corpus (YELC), which was collected in 2011 by Yonsei University in Korea. It consists of two types of writing, which consists of 6,572 argumentative and narrative compositions. Out of this collection, 3,286 argumentative writings were selected for this study, which contains 728,183 words. The reason I selected YELC for the analysis is that this corpus consists of a large number of writings and that it is free data open to researchers although the writings were collected from a specific university (Yonsei).

The argumentative writings concern topics relating to social issues (the pros and cons on smoking in public places, anonymity of the internet, mandatory military service, corporal punishment in school, animal testing, and using a mobile phone while driving). The topics were randomly assigned to each student. The essays in YELC had already been assessed and classified by native English faculty instructors in the College English Department at Yonsei University. The proficiency bands in the placement test range from A1 to C2[1].

The reference data is LOCNESS[1], an acronym of Louvain Corpus of Native English Essays, which includes four types of essays: 1) 149,574 words of argumentative essays written by American university students, 2) 18,826 words of literary-mixed essays written by American University students, 3) 59,568 words of argumentative and literary essays written by British university students, and 4) 60,209 words of British A-level argumentative essays. I chose argumentative types of writings as academic writings as academic writings because this genre requires coherence use logical connectors.

I eliminated three groups of essays in this corpus: one group of literary-mixed essays written by American University students and two groups of literary essays written by British university students (one is a mixed collection of literary and expository essays and the other of literary essays only). The two corpora are compared in terms of the number of words and number of texts in Table 1 below.

---

[1] LOCNESS is a corpus of native English essays comprised of British pupils' A-level essays (totaling 60,209 words), British university students' essays (totaling 95,695 words), and American university students' essays (totaling 168,400 words). The total number of words is 324,304.

Table 7.1 Corpus Size for YELC

Study Corpus	YELC	LOCNESS
Number of Words	728,183	228,802*
Number of Texts	3286	226

*Note: The number of words indicates that of selected essays for this study.

The reference corpus, LOCNESS is small compared to YELC. Therefore, I will compare the frequencies across two corpora by the percent of each category.

Analysis

This study uses both a quantitative method and a qualitative method. *Antconc 3.4.3* was employed as a corpus tool for a quantitative analysis in order to reveal the frequencies of LBs and for a qualitative analysis to investigate the concordances for each LB across the two corpora. For the target bundle, four-word LBs will be retrieved because they are "the most researched length for writing studies" (Ädel & Erman 2012; Chen & Baker 2010; Cortes 2004).

As for cut-off and dispersion criteria, I set my own levels to account for the different data size compared to previous studies. For example, previous cut-off criteria have been at a frequency of twenty-five times per million words (Chen & Baker 2010) and dispersion criteria at nine texts per million words (Ädel & Erman 2012). For this study, I set nineteen times as the cut-off criterion and five texts as the dispersion criterion for YELC. For LOCNESS, I set five times as the cut-off criterion and four texts as the dispersion criterion, as shown in Table 2.

Table 7.2 Cut-off and Dispersion Criteria

Corpora	Cut-off Criteria	Dispersion Criteria
YELC	19 times	15 texts
LOCNESS	5 times	4 texts

Next, I removed some bundles which are irrelevant to the analysis, as done in studies by Chen & Baker (2010) and Ädel & Erman (2012). I eliminated topic-specific bundles, content bundles with proper nouns, bundles composed exclusively of function words, bundles of function words and topic-specific words, contraction forms (includes non-contraction forms), interviews, meaningless bundles, and fragments of other bundles based on the adapted criteria from Salazar (2011) in Table 3.

Table 7.3 Exclusion Criteria (adapted from Salazar, 2011)

Topic-specific bundles	*the extension of a, jaw and the lips the university of California, the two-way ANOVA*
Bundles composed exclusively of function words	*as in b the, as in a or, et al and the, of # with #*
Bundles of function words and topic-specific words	*of the speaker s; from the speaker s*
Content bundles with Proper nouns	*the university of California, the two-way ANOVA*
Contraction forms	*don t have to, I think it s, don t know i*
Interviews	*I think it s, don t want to*
Meaningless bundles	*nan emm nan emm, et al s study*
Fragments of other bundles	*the scope of this, been shown to be, degree to which they*

Through the process of the refinement outlined above, 412 types of LBs were retrieved from YELC, and 79 types of LBs were extracted from LOCNESS. The types and the tokens of each corpus are displayed in Table 4. The numbers in parentheses are normalized frequencies.

Table 7.4 The Normalized and Raw Types and the Tokens in two corpora

Corpus	Types Raw Frequency (per 10000 wds)	Tokens Raw Frequency (per 10000 wds)
YELC	412 (58)	15115 (20757)
LOCNESS	79 (345)	763 (3334)

Results and Discussions

Frequencies of LBs

The non-native data YELC showed 412 types of LBs in raw frequency and the native corpus LOCNESS displayed 79 types of LBs under the same criteria. However, the two corpora include different numbers of words (728,183 in YELC and 228,802 in LOCNESS). Therefore, I compare the normalized frequencies between the two corpora after converting them from the raw frequencies. The results reveal that YELC produced 58 types and 20,757 tokens of LBs and that LOCNESS produced 345 types and 3,334 tokens of LBs. I normalized the frequencies per 10,000 words. Types and tokens in YELC and LOCNESS are shown in Table 5 below.

Table 7.5 The Types and the Tokens in YELC and LOCNESS

	YELC (per 10000 wds)	LOCNESS (per 10000 wds)
Types	58	345
Tokens	20,757	3,334

The findings indicate that NS students deployed a much greater variety of types of LBs (345 vs. 58), whereas Korean EFL students employed larger numbers of LBs in terms of tokens (20,257 versus 3,334), which is in line with Yoon and Choi's (2015) results. The result also aligns with findings in Ädel & Erman (2012) and Chen & Baker (2010).

Structural classification of LBs

The first research question is about the frequencies, the commonalities and differences in terms of structural classifications between the two corpora. I adopted the structural frame from Biber et al. (1999). Figure 1 shows the distribution of LBs in the two corpora based on structural classification. Table 6 displays the distribution of LBs across subcategories in each structural category.

The Figure 1 indicates that the two corpora show slightly different distributions, whereas the order of the three structural categories is the same between the two groups: in YELC, VP (82%) > NP (7%) > PP (7%, rounded) > OTHERS (6%) and, in LOCNESS, VP (52%) > NP (27%) > PP (17%) > OTHERS (6%).

Fig. 7.1 Distribution of LBs in Structural Classification across YELC and LOCNESS

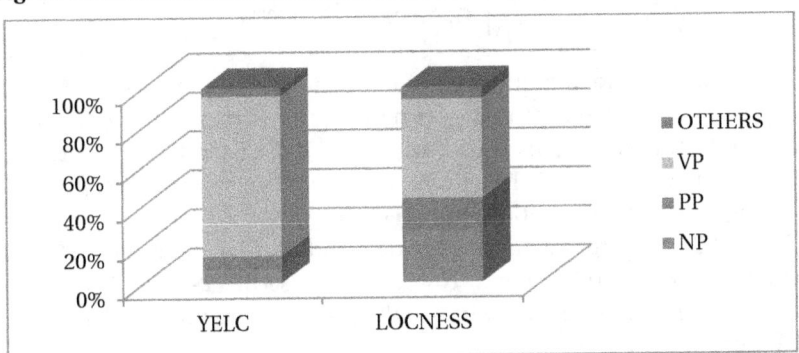

Table 6 shows that there are slight differences between the frequencies of NP-based LBs and PP-based LBs across the two corpora (7% and 7% in YELC, and 27% and 17% in LOCNESS respectively).

Table 7.6. Structural classification of LBs in YELC (Biber et al., 1999)

Category	Subcategory	Frequency (Types)		Examples
		YELC	LOCNESS	
NP-based		30 (7%)	22 (27%)	*a lot of people*
PP-based		28 (7%)	13 (17%)	*for these reasons I*
VP-based	Copula *be* + NP/AdjP	69 (17%)	6 (7.7%)	*there are lots of* / *is one of the*
	VP with active verb	152 (37%)	7 (8.8%)	*don't have any* / *have a lot of*
	Anticipatory *it* + VP/AdjP + complement clause	20 (5%)	3 (3.9%)	*it is true that* / *it is important to*
	Passive verb + PP fragment	32 (8%)	1 (1.3%)	*should not be allowed* / *can be seen as*
	(VP +) *that*-clause fragment	13 (3%)	7 (8.8%)	*that all Korean men* / *that it is not*
	(V/Adj +) *to*-clause fragment	4 (1%)	4 (5.1%)	*to be a good* / *to be able to*
	Others	49 (11%)	13 (16.4%)	*when they are driving* / *I do not think*
	VP in total	339 (82%)	41 (52%)	
Others		15 (4%)	3 (6%)	*As you can see*
Total		412 (100%)	79 (100%)	

In addition, it shows that the relative frequency between types of LBs in the two groups, i.e., the native and non-native groups is not that different. In other words, the two groups show similar usage of LBs in terms of structural classification: VP > NP > PP. This order of usage reflects the writers' proficiency in English academic writing. In other words, NNSs' most frequent use of VP-based LBs converges with the previous studies (Chen & Baker 2010; Biber et al. 1999). On the other hand, NS' frequent use of VP-based LBs showed somewhat different result compared to the previous literatures (Ädel & Erman 2012; Biber et al. 1999).

Functional classification of LBs

Table 7 shows the distribution of function classifications across the two groups of writers. The classification is adapted from Biber et al. (2004). According to Table 7, the observed distribution of LBs in YELC shows "other" types of LBs to be the largest (58%), followed by stance bundles (38%), referential bundles (2.6%), and discourse organizers (0.4%). In this study, the category "Special Conversation" was not included for the analysis because no uses of it were found. Functionally, the distribution of uses of LBs in LOCNESS is as follows: reference expression bundles are the largest (47%), followed by others (28%), then stance expression bundles (24%), and then discourse organizers (1%).

Concerning Research Question 3, the results across two corpora were similar to the previous findings in their structural classification distributions but the findings in the NS' students' corpus indicated different traits from results in the previous studies (Ädel & Erman 2012; Chen & Baker 2010).

Table 7.7. Functional Classification of LBs in YELC and LOCNESS

Categories	Sub-Category			Types		Examples
				YELC	LOCNESS	
1) Stance Expressions	Epistemic			56 (20%)	5 (26%)	I think all Koreans, t is true that, it is not true
	Attitude/ modality stance	Desire		7 (4.3%)	2 (11%)	I don't want to I don't like
		Obligation		84 (50%)	5 (26%)	Must use their real
		Intention/ prediction		0 (0%)	2 (11%)	Is going to be-
		Ability		9 (5.7%)	5 (26%)	But we can't
Subtotal				156 (38%)	19 (24%)	
2) Discourse Organizers	Topic introduction/focus			1 (50%)	0 (0%)	On the following reasons
	Topic elaboration/ clarification			1 (50%)	1 (100%)	On the other hand
Subtotal				2 (0.4%)	1 (1%)	
3) Referential Expressions	Identification/focus			2 (18%)	16 (43.3%)	What I want to
	Specification of attributes	Quantity		5 (45%)	4 (10.8%)	A lot of money there are lots of
		Intangible Framing		3 (27%)	13 (35.1%)	When it comes to On top of

	Time/ place/ text reference	1 (10%)	4 (10.8%)	At the same time As a result the As a result of
Subtotal		11 (2.6%)		37 (47%)
4) Others	Existence Evaluation Writer's stance	243 (58%)	22 (28%)	There are many people It is hard to, It is very dangerous I agree with the, I agree that people, I disagree with the, I disagree that people

In contrast, findings are quite different from the previous literature in their distribution of functional classification. These results reflect two groups of writers' traits in two groups. The details will be talked about it in the discussion section. The different distributions of functional classification between the two groups of writers are shown in Figure 2.

Fig. 7.2 Distribution of LBs in Functional Classification across YELC and LOCNESS

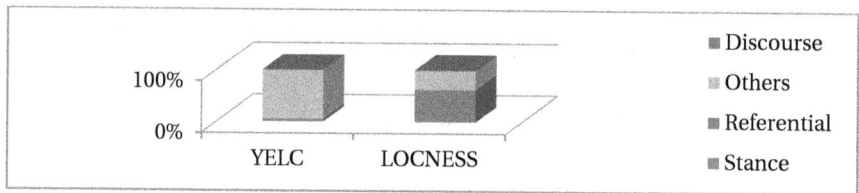

Discussion

The two groups showed the same usage of LBs in terms of structural classification: VP > NP > PP. This reflects the two writer groups' traits - Korean college students and American-British college students: 1) college students' inexpertise compared to scholars' expertise in writings, in the previous studies which studied published academic research articles (Hyland 2008a; Hyland 2008b; Chen & Baker 2010). This result is slightly different from that in the previous literature (Biber et al. 1999; Ädel & Erman 2012; Chen & Baker 2010).

Structural classification of LB uses reveals that VP-based bundles were frequently used with modal verbs in YELC. Also, strong stance modals such as **should, have to, and must** were highly used, which indicates that the NNSs' low English writing proficiency as the following.

(1) *Non-smokers also dangerous to breathe gas of burning side of tobacco that has critical materials which attack similar organs of smokers. Last reason why it **should** be banned is anti-economical.* (YELC, 408)

(2) *I think physical punishment **should** not be allowed in all schools. I have a three different reasons about why we **should** not allow the physical punishment in school.* (YELC, 409)

(3) *Yes we **should** use animals in medical experiments. Because, the life of man have to be more protected than that of animals.* (YELC, 410)

(4) *Citizens have liberty of their own. So they need not smell the disgusting smoking smell. But we **have to** consider smoker's will to smoke.* (YELC, 460)

(5) *We knows military service is unfair and uneffective. even If we takes much time solve this problems, we **have to** change military service (Before i go military service).* (YELC, 473)

(6) *But we **have to** know there are also some side effects of that privacy. I can name two side effects in here.* (YELC, 482)

(7) *If there are chance to kill person smoking in public area **must** be banned. I think smoking in all public building is very selish behavior. I admit that smokers want to smoke. but non smokers don't want to smoke. If smokers desperately want to smoke then they **must** go outside and smoke in the place nobody exist.* (YELC, 407)

(8) *If military service is not forced, few would volunteer for army. This will lead the erosion of self-defence of South Korea, which can trigger the invasion of North Korea. Therefore, we **must** complete military service not only to save ourselves but also to save our country, Republic of Korea.* (YELC, 435)

(9) *Some people who have weak mind sometimes suicide. Because this situation, we **must** use our real name on the internet.* (YELC, 455)

Another interesting finding in the NNS' corpus is that Korean learners of English employed 2nd person pronoun *you* and indefinite pronoun phrases *most people/some people* in the excerpts (10) and (11). This might reflect Korean EFL writers' tone-down claim to express their stance.

(10) *If **you** imagine the elementary school in Chosun Dynasty, what are the things appear in your mind? **Most people** would say a stick that teachers usually carry with them to punish students. **Some people** might state that the world has changed, so the allowance of physical punishment should be vanished.* (YELC, 368)

(11) **Some people** say that people don't have to use their real name on the Internet, because if people have to use their real name, the users of the Internet can't express their opinions freely. However, I strongly believe that people have to use real name on-line. (YELC, 369)

As for functional classifications, the observed distribution of LBs in YELC and in LOCNESS showed quite different aspects: the quite highly distribution of stance bundles (38%) implies that Korean college learners do not notice the register awareness (written vs. spoken and academic vs. non-academic) and that they regard stance bundles as a strategy of showing their opinion.

There are other two stance constructions in the two corpora as the following:

(12) *Animals are used in many medical experiment now days. i love cat , dog, dolphin and many animals. so **I think** we **must** protect animals from using animals in medical experiment. but, we cannot experiment with trees and flowers* (YELC, 10)

(13) ***I think** smoking **must** be banned in all public buildings. Surely someone thinks that smokers have the right of freedom that they smoke anywhere.* (YELC, 2909)

(14) *What is marijuana? It is a plant, and **I think** it **should be** legalized.* (LOCNESS, USARG)

(15) ***I think** that I **would like to** see a change in the law to allow women to have children if they feel able to cope but I feel if legalised it would be a decision taken to freely by women and not taking into consideration the consequences.* (LOCNESS, Alevels8)

The first stance construction is *I think*: this construction in (12) to (15) are used with the strongest auxiliary (*must*) in YELC and less strong auxiliary (*should, would like to*) in LOCNESS. This result indicates that NNS overused strong modals even with VP constructions although native writers use less strong modal expressions.

The second stance structure is *I +adverb +believe+ that* phrase: this has various types of adverbs between the subject person pronoun *I* and the lexical mental verb *believe* as the excerpts in (16) through (25).

(16) *Some people say that people don't have to use their real name on the Internet, because if people have to use their real name, the users of the Internet can't express their opinions freely. However, **I strongly believe that** people have to use real name on-line.* (YELC, 369)

(17) *In conclusion,* **I firmly believe that** *physical punishment must be stopped in all scools because first, students are also humans like teachers, who wants to be treated more gently, and second, there is a variety of better ways to punish students.* (YELC, 72)

(18) *Likewise, Smoking can cause big accidents. In conclusion,* **I definitely believe that** *smoking should be banned in all public buildings for those reasons.* (YELC, 1792)

(19) *In conclusion,* **I wholeheartedly believe that** *the physical punishment of children in schools is only a selfish method which is invented by teachers who want to push children to study more easily.* (YELC, 2219)

(20) *In conclusion,* **I largely believe that** *people must use their real name on the Internet. One reason for this is that it can play morally positive roles. Moreover It enable us to have find somone's new great aspects in real life. Therefore the advantages of using real name outweigh its disadvantages.* (YELC, 2769)

(21) **I myself believe that** *fox hunting should be banned as it is very cruel.* (LOCNESS, Alevel3)

(22) **I personally believe that** *the agricultural industry will never collapse, due to the common agricultural policy (CAP), and price support by the government.* (LOCNESS, Alevel7)

(23) *Yet despite all the atrocities he commits, I don't believe the audience ever really hates Caligula and* **I do believe that** *Camus manages to evoke both sympathy and admiration for him.* (LOCNESS, BRSUR1)

(24) **I firmly believe that** *the advent of 1992 will result in a loss of sovereignty for Britain. This loss need not however be negative. In fact, in political, economic and defence terms I feel this realocation of resources can and will be very positive.* (LOCNESS, BRSUR3)

(25) *If my cousin did have the child, it would have caused problems because she was pregnant for a twenty-two year old married man.* **I still believe** *she should have been forced to go through with the pregnancy.* (LOCNESS, USARG)

As can be seen from the above excerpts, NNS and NS' corpora showed different distributions. Korean student writers mainly used strong adverbs, such as *strongly, firmly, wholeheartedly, definitely,* and *largely,* while native English student writers primarily employed less strong adverbs, e.g., *firmly, personally, still,* and other words, such as *myself* (reflexive pronoun) and auxiliary *do.* The finding also reveals that NNSs are likely to prefer strong expressions rather than hedges. Table 8 displays the distributions stance phrase structures with adverbs in the two corpora.

Table 8. Distributions of Stance phrase structures, "I +ADVERB+believe+that" in YELC & LOCNESS

Phrase structure (I + ADVERB + believe+ that)	YELC Raw (per 10000wds)	LOCNESS Raw (per 10000wds)
I + STRONGLY + believe + that	53	0
I + FIRMLY + believe + that	16	1
I + WHOLEHEARTEDLY + believe + that	2	0
I + however + believe + that	2	0
I + DEFINITELY + believe + that	1	0
I + LARGELY + believe + that	1	0
I + ALSO + believe + that	1	0
I + MYSELF + believe + that	0	1
I + PERSONALLY + believe + that	0	2
I + do + believe + that	0	1
I + STILL + believe + that	0	1
Total	76 (1.04)	6 (0.26)

According to Table 8, *I +ADVERB+believe+that* structure showed different distributions in YELC and LOCNESS. I also compared the three stance constructions in Table 9.

Table 9. Three Stance phrases, "I think," "I believe" & "I * believe" structures in YELC & LOCNESS

Phrase structure	YELC Raw (per 10000wds)	LOCNESS Raw (per 10000wds)
I think	3587 (49.25)	80 (3.49)
I believe	155 (2.12)	47 (2.05)
I * believe	76 (1.04)	6 (0.26)
Total	3908 (53.6)	133 (5.81)

According to Table 9, *I think, I believe,* and *I * believe* constructions were quite frequently used in YELC compared to LOCNESS although these structures can be found in LOCNESS.

In YELC, *I think* construction showed the highest use, *I believe* displayed the second one, and *I* plus a few other words (*adverbs, auxiliaries*) plus *believe* did last. The writings in LOCNESS showed similar distribution. However, the normalized frequency (49.25 vs. 3.49) in the two corpora displayed a big difference, which observes that Korean learners overused *I think* construction and they regarded the construction as a strategy for showing their stance

(Kim 2013; Hong 2013; Hong 2015). In particular, the college writers in the two corpora used *I think* construction with the auxiliary stance expressions, such as *must, should,* and *would like to*.

Following the research questions, I discuss overall in regard to the three main issues. Regarding PP-based bundles, Korean learners are less likely to use PP-based bundles (7% vs. 17%). One difference between the NSs and the NNSs is in the presence of "lexical teddy bears" (Hasselgren. 1994). This refers to a NNS's reliance on a familiar term or expression by "choosing words and phrases closely resembling their L1 or those learnt early or widely used" (Hasselgren 1994, 237). In addition, NS' writers frequent use of VP-based LBs might reflect their inexpertise in academic writings, compared to expert writings, e.g., scholars. This finding seems interesting compared to the previous studies (Ädel & Erman 2012; Biber et al. 1999) and is necessary to study in the next research. As for NP-based bundles, Korean learners were the least frequently used (7% vs. 27%). This result shows that writers display a lack of register awareness (NP-based bundles are frequently used in academic writings) at the early stages of proficiency development. In terms of functional classification of LBs, the study reveals the use of few discourse organizers in the NS and NNS corpus. The results are contrary to those found in Ädel & Erman (2012).

However, a higher number of stance expressions found in the NNSs' data partly supports findings of the previous literature (Yang 2017; Yoon & Choi 2015). This result also indicates that non-native students display their stance in a strong and direct way (using strong modals) in argumentative writings. Reluctance to the use of hedges also substantiates the earlier findings, that is, that NNSs are less likely to use hedges, favoring instead strong and direct language (Ädel & Erman 2012; Chen & Baker 2010).

Conclusion

This study investigated the use of four-word LBs. The mixed-method approach of quantitative and qualitative analyses revealed that NNSs displayed more frequent and various uses of LBs than NSs (NNS used fewer different types while the number of tokens was larger in NNS' data than in NS'corpus). LBs in YELC were classified into structural patterns and functional ones. Structurally, the LBs were classified based on Biber et al., (1999). VP-based was the most frequently occurring classification, followed by NP-based, others, and PP-based. This supports Chen & Baker's (2010) results by revealing that the NNSs show a tendency to prefer VP-based bundles to NP-based ones. Surprisingly, the NS' college students' corpus showed the similar distribution pattern.

Functionally, I classified LBs based on Biber's (2006) categories. Stance expressions were highly used in the NNS' compositions while referential bundles were mostly employed in the NS' writings. This result confirms the results found in the previous research. Most of all, the findings were distinctive in that only a few discourse organizers appeared, while a number of stance expressions were found in the NNS' writings. Notably, most of the stance bundles they employed consisted of strong and direct language. In Adel & Erman (2012), discourse organizers occupied the largest proportion in the NNS writings, which stands in clear contrast to the current study's findings. Stance bundles have previously been observed to be the scarcer in NNS writings, which also marks a slight difference from this study. However, it confirms earlier findings that NNSs are less likely to use hedges (Adel & Erman 2012; Chen & Baker 2010).

The findings suggest that Korean EFL learners need to be taught to focus more on their writing as an essay rather than a combination of discrete paragraphs. For example, students are required to practice discourse organizers during their writing classes. Also, it is useful to teach students for English for Special Purposes (ESP) using Academic Formulas List (AFL) for phraseology derived from various disciplines proposed by Simpson & Ellis (2010). NNS' traits of ungrammatical uses of LBs and less use of discourse organizers suggests pedagogical implications in how to teach grammar and coherence in writing. Moreover, they propose the next step to ESP pedagogy such as enhancing genre awareness (e.g., argumentative/narrative, science, engineering, humanities, etc.). In addition, ungrammatical uses of LBs indicate a need for greater emphasis on grammar instruction. Moreover, overuse of strong modals suggests that classroom instruction on the use of hedges is especially necessary to Korean EFL students.

References

Ädel, A., Erman, B. 2012. Recurrent word combinations in academic writing by native and non-native speakers of English: A lexical bundles approach. *English for Specific Purposes, 31*(2), 81-92.

Allen, D. 2009. Lexical Bundles in Learner Writing: An Analysis of Formulaic Language in the ALESS Learner Corpus. *Komaba Journal of English Education*, 107-127.

Altenberg, B. 1998. On the phraseology of spoken English: The evidence of recurrent word combinations. In A. P.Cowie (Ed.), *Phraseology: Theory,Analysis and Applications* (pp.101-122). Oxford: Oxford University Press.

Bell, D. M. 2004. Correlative and non-correlative "*on the other hand.*" *Journal of Pragmatics, 36*(12), 2179-2184.

Biber, D., Barbieri, F. 2007. Lexical bundles in university spoken and written registers. *English for Specific Purposes, 26*(3). 263-286.

Biber, D. 2006. Stance in spoken and written university registers. *Journal of English for Academic Purposes, 5*(2), 97-116.

Biber, D., Conrad, S., & Cortes, V. 2004. If you look at: Lexical bundles in university teaching and textbooks. *Applied Linguistics, 25*(3), 371–405.

Biber, D. Johansson, S., Leech, G. Conrad, S., Finegan, E. F. 1999. *Longman grammar of spoken and written English*. London: Longman.

Chen, Y. & Baker, P. 2010. Lexical bundles in L1 and L2 academic writing. *Language Learning and Technology, 14*(2), 30–49.

Choi, B. 2015. Lexical bundles in linguistic research articles: a comparative study of native and non-native writing. Unpublished Master Thesis. Department of English Language and Literature. Seoul National University. Korea.

Cortes, V. 2004. Lexical bundles in published and student disciplinary writing: Examples from history and biology. *English for Specific Purposes 23*(4), 397-434.

Cortes, V. 2006. Teaching Lexical Bundles in the disciplines: An example from a writing intensive history class. *Linguistics and Education. 17*(4), 391-406.

Hasselgren, A. 1994. Lexical teddy bears and advanced learners: a study into the ways Norwegian students cope with English vocabulary. *International Journal of Applied Linguistics, 4*(2). 237-260.

Hoffman, C. 2000. The spread of English and the growth of multilingualism with English in Europe. In J.Cenoz & U.Jessner (Eds.), *English in Europe: The Acquisition of a Third Language (pp.1-21)*. Clevedon: Multilingual Matters.

Hong, S. 2013. An n-gram analysis of Korean English learners' writing. *Korean Journal of English Language and Linguistics. 13*(2), 313-336.

Hong, S. 2015. The comparison of n-gram use between intermediate and advanced *Korean learners of English. Journal of Language Sciences. 22*(1), 147-170.

Hyland, K. 2008a. Academic clusters: Text patterning in published and post graduate writing. *International Journal of Applied Linguistics, 18*(1), 41–62.

Hyland, K. 2008b. As can be seen: Lexical bundles and disciplinary variation. *English for Specific Purposes, 27*(1), 4-21.

Kim, J. 2013. Lexical Bundles in Korean colleges' English essays: A corpus-based comparative study. *English language and Literature Teaching. 19*(3), 157-179.

Kwon, Y. and Lee E. 2014. Lexical bundles in the Korean EFL teacher talk corpus: A comparison between non-native and native English teachers. *The Journal of Asia TEFL. 11*(3), 73-103.

Lee, E. 2009. A corpus-based study of the Korean EFL learners use of formulaic sequences. *Foreign Language Education. 16*(2), 321-340.

Lee, S. 2012. A study on the use of lexical bundles in science journals Korean National Research Foundation.

Lindquist, H. 2009. *Corpus linguistics and the description of English*. Edinburgh University Press.

McCulley, G. 1985. Writing quality, coherence, and cohesion. *Research in the Teaching of English. 19*(3), 269-282.

Rhee, S. C. and Jung, C. K. 2014. Compilation of the Yonsei English Learner Corpus (YELC) 2011 and Its Use for Understanding Current Usage of English by Korean Pre-university Students. *Journal of Korea Contents Association. 14*(11), 1019-1029.

Romer, U. 2009. English in academia: Does nativeness matter? *Anglistik: International Journal of English Studies, 20*(2), 89–100.

Salazar, D. 2011. Lexical bundles in scientific English: A corpus-based study of native and non-native writing. Unpublished doctoral dissertation. Universitat de Barcelona, Spain.

Schimmit, N. (ed.) 2004. *Formulaic Sequences.* Amsterdam: Benjamins.

Schimmit, N. (ed.) 2010. *Research Vocabulary.* Palgrave, Macmillan.

Simpson, V. R. & Ellis, N. C. 2010. An Academic Formulas List: New Methods in Phraseology Research. *Applied Linguistics. 31*(4), 487-512.

Scott, M. & Tribble, C. 2006. *Textual Patterns.* Amsterdam: Benjamins.

Stubbs, M. 2007. An example of frequent English phraseology: Distribution, structures and functions. In R. Facchinetti (Ed.), *Corpus Linguistics 25 Years On* (pp. 89–105). Amsterdam: Rodop.

Wells, G. 2002. The Centrality of Talk in Education. In K. Nor,an (ed.), *Thinking voices: The work of the national oracy project.* London: Hodder and Stoughton.

Wray, A. 2002. Formulaic sequences in second language teaching: Principle and practice. *Applied Linguistics. 21*, 463-489.

Yang, Y. 2017. Lexical Bundles in Argumentative and Narrative Writings by Chinese EFL Learners. *International Journal of English Linguistics. 7*(3), 58-69.

Yoon, C. & Choi, J. 2015. Lexical Bundles in Korean University Students' EFL Compositions: A Comparative Study of Register and Use. *Modern English Education, 16*(3), 47-69.

CHAPTER EIGHT

Integrating Biblical and Historical Precedent Units Awareness in Teaching ESP in Terms of Media Discourse

Svetlana Rubtsova

Relevance of cultural awareness

The issue of incorporating cultural knowledge awareness both in ESP and translation studies curricula is vital for facilitating intercultural/multicultural/cross-cultural/linguacultural skills of graduates that will guarantee them successful professional communication in their future jobs across cultures. Multiculturalism is one of the most significant transferable skills for present-day graduates, enabling them to work successfully in various cultural environments. The theory of intercultural communication has been entertaining serious attention on the part of linguists, theoreticians of translation, ESP teachers, pragmatists, sociologists, cognitivists, not to mention psychologists. This interest is boosted by globalization and internationalization of education, science, and research. The importance of incorporating cross-cultural awareness in modern languages curricula is universally recognized.

As language plays an important part in professional and intercultural communication intensified by the Internet and other new technologies, mastering foreign languages and primarily English as lingua franca is crucial for specialists in the sphere of sciences and humanities. However, it is not sufficient to be a fluent speaker, gaining proficiency in the phonology, grammar, lexis, etc. of a certain language. According to Bennett (1997), it is also necessary to avoid being a "fluent fool", meaning there are other important aspects of knowledge essential for successful communication. A modern language speaker/ translator/ interpreter is supposed to combine foreign language expertise and skills with being able to understand, feel and assess the target language cultural connotations. This ability refers to the intercultural/cross-cultural/multicultural competence. A multicultural speaker/ translator/ interpreter is a mediator between 'cultural knowledge frameworks' and 'cultural practices' (Byram 1997, 64).

Michael Byram (1997), Claire Kramsch (1993) and others argue that it is important to promote the ideal of the intercultural speaker. That is, one who possesses:

1. intercultural communicative competence as a complex entity of intercultural relations;
2. background knowledge in both target and home cultures and languages;
3. critical cultural awareness which comprises abilities to evaluate perspectives, practices, and products of both cultures. (Byram, 1997)

Evidently, this is also true of translators and interpreters.

Linguacultural content

This paper focuses on the second aspect as previously stated - the background knowledge in target and home cultures with the focus on precedent units with historical and biblical allusions, which constitute a solid part of the national thesaurus referring to culture in any language. The process of cross-language communication and translation is not just a matter of comprehending the meaning of a discourse or rendering it from one language into another. It also presupposes rendering from the home culture into the target one or the other way round. Such language units from the cultural thesaurus of a language as popular lines from poetry, nursery rhymes or songs, quotes from films, television shows, citations from literary works, political and advertisement slogans, titles of books and films, proverbs, etc. are called precedent units/phenomena/texts or intertextual units. They are part of linguacultural background knowledge of a native speaker. They are normally well known and in common use. Every language has a certain set of nationally specific and universal/global precedent units. Thanks to the process of globalization, accelerated by the Internet and mass media, many national precedent units become universal, while in the good old times that was possible only thanks to popular literary works and successful translations thereof. Universal/global precedent units refer to linguacultural information across nationalities. Proper names turned into appellative names, phraseological units of biblical origin and those rooting back to works of the world literature, catchphrases from the Ancient Greek and Roman mythology, prominent citations of historical and political figures constitute a certain universal 'cultural luggage' or 'cultural code' of a native speaker. Besides, native speakers possess specific knowledge in terms of their national culture reflecting the world-image of their home language and culture – a national 'cultural code'. In teaching and learning foreign languages both universal and national precedent units should be under scrutiny for students to become skilled and competent speakers/translators/interpreters possessing not only professional but also cross-cultural communication skills. In this respect, biblical and historical precedent units are of particular interest, because they clearly demonstrate the unity and the diversity of cultures from the perspective of rendering 'bits' of cultural background knowledge information from one language into another. Precedent units and texts are widely used in political media discourse. Sometimes they are difficult to translate/interpret and can occlude comprehension in case of the lack of linguacultural knowledge. For this reason, the syllabus of the additional educational program "Translation in the sphere of professional communication" (the tertiary level of education) at St Petersburg State University includes a special discipline "Intercultural communication from the perspective of translation". It is aimed at facilitating intercultural competence as regards tracing allusions and analyzing metaphors, mastering catchphrases from myths and legends and quotes from Shakespeare, as well as those related to the world history, the Bible, etc. Such linguacultural content is of crucial importance and as a rule evokes great interest among students.

Biblical and historical allusions in political media discourse

Media discourse in general and political media discourse, in particular, contribute to the intensification of communication across borders in the context of intensive informational and scientific exchange that brings people of different cultures together. It is evident that political media discourse plays an especially important role in developing languages and broadening knowledge, politics, and issues referring to them being one of the main domains of international communication thanks to the mutual interest of representatives of different cultures to common issues of humanity. On the other hand, it is thanks to the world mass media that national cultural background knowledge is getting across borders and cultures, thus becoming in its turn global. That is, mass media helps in a way disseminate cultural knowledge with the help of political media discourse. On top of that, being for the most part rather emotive and often metaphorical, political media discourse, as a rule, abounds in catchphrases, buzzwords, citations and clichés that constitute the linguacultural thesaurus of a native speaker. Proper comprehension of the notional and emotional implications of political media discourse in the target language is essential for successful intercultural communication. The sources of precedent units/texts are literature, cinematography, television, songs, mythology, history, to name but a few, which makes the learning process really challenging and entertaining at the same time. Some of precedent units stay in common use, others turn into old-fashioned lexis or 'pass into nothingness' with time. Political media discourse in general and speeches of politicians, in particular, are frequently Aesopian: full of hints, allusions and implications, and inferring the underlying logic thereof sometimes similar to the process of deciphering encrypted information. Textual and intertextual complicated correlations become visible in the process of analyzing the meaning of precedent units. Visualization of cultural information through the Internet, cinema, television and social networking enlarges and internationalizes the corpus of precedent units present in the lexicon of every language.

Precedent units/texts such as quotes and catchphrases dating back to biblical parables and historical events are an inherent part of both global and national cultural codes of a native speaker (Rubtsova: 2005). Biblical phrases relate to universal precedent units, at least, in terms of Christian cultures. Nevertheless, certain difficulties of comprehension and translation can arise even in the Christian cultural context, because all languages (the English and the Russian languages for this instance) reflect the world differently and have somewhat different images of it. Interestingly, Biblical precedent units, being widely used in most European countries and both Americas, provide an example of a certain dissimilarity between the cultural background knowledge of English and Russian speakers, with the level of their awareness of biblical metaphors and allusions being far from equal. This discrepancy might well be accounted for by the infamous political events in Russia in the 20th century. While Russian newspapers of the 19th century were replete with biblical phrases after the revolution of 1917 for more than 70 years religion and religious lexis were expunged from the minds of people, textbooks, and mass media. Only thanks to classical Russian literature and clandestinely maintained religious traditions in family circles, did some biblical phrases remain in general use, frequently though losing their original stylistic connotations and turning into humorous or even sarcastic rather than pathetic-oratorical ones – a phenomenon that can be called 'genre reduction'. These days, though, there is a certain renaissance in this respect – quite a few newspapers, television presenters, and politicians use biblical phrases willingly because they make political discourse rather eloquent and oblique. Apart from this quantitative difference, there are certain qualitative ones. Thanks to the fact that every language has its own image of the world and segments the reality differently, there are incongruities in reinterpreting and rethinking biblical narratives and biblical phrases in both languages. For instance, some biblical allusions and metaphors have become precedent units only in one of the languages or there is only a partial overlapping of meanings/ connotations in both target and home languages. A proficient speaker/ translator/ interpreter should have a profound knowledge of the main corpus of such precedent units in both languages and of their translation equivalents, if any, or be good at finding other relevant ways of rendering the main meaning and as many additional connotations as possible from one language into another.

Modified historical or biblical precedent units

One of the stylistic devices of political discourse is a quasi-citation. Quasi-citation is an intendedly modified/transformed citation of some idiomatic expressions or catchphrases. Modified precedent units make political media discourse rather eloquent and are able to generate a wide range of associations: *"This vision of being my brother's keeper has important political and social consequences when it comes to such issues as healthcare, consumer protection or education reform,"* Siker said at the meeting. (Los Angeles Times, 14 August 2010). The original biblical phrase "Am I my brother's keeper?" has several implications, such as refusal to take responsibility for someone, desire to conceal murder, etc. The following possible chain of associations can be reconstructed - this is the claim to take on responsibility for healthcare (contrary to the presupposed negation of the original precedent unit), hence - not to do so would be treacherous and criminal, like murdering one's own brother... and so on. For every recipient the association chain can be longer or shorter, refer to some other aspects of this biblical parable and have somewhat different emotive tinges depending on the emotional responsiveness, imagination, associative abilities and other personal traits of character of the recipient, and last but not least, his/her educational and social background.

Curiously, quite a few titles of books, films, computer games, newspaper articles have titles of biblical origin, because some biblical phrases are rather concise and succinct, at the same time being rich both in semantic and emotive connotations. According to Safire, "The Bible is a hot source of the latest titles." (Safire 1993). Such titles of books, films, computer games and popular songs give a new birth to some obsolete precedent units with historical or biblical allusions. This refers to another function of precedent texts/units - the function of 'reminding' or the reminiscent function, i.e., evoking certain allusions to some other precedent unit, which is usually the case with titles of books and films. If the film or the book in question is popular enough to have a certain lasting emotional influence upon a big enough community, its title can bring an out-of-use biblical phrase or an almost forgotten historical name back into common use. Sometimes such precedent unit can take on a new emotive connotation and start evoking new associations or in the process of translating - even a bit different meaning in a different culture. For instance, the title of a well-known novel by E. Hemingway "For Whom the Bell Tolls" is a line from John Donn's poem: "Therefore, send not to know / For whom the bell tolls, / It tolls for thee." Curiously, in the Russian version of the title the presupposition evident for native speakers - other people's death cannot help influencing one's life ("Each man's death diminishes me, / For I am involved in mankind") - is not explicit. This implication is lost in the Russian translation, though it certainly makes the meaning of the title in its English version philosophically more profound and more tragic. This example demonstrates the fact that even in grammatically and semantically correct translations some "losses" are inevitable (Retsker 2007). In the instance mentioned above, it is a certain linguacultural connotation valid for native speakers that is "untranslatable".

Modifications can be contextual (situational), lexical and syntactic (Leppihalme 1997; Rubtsova 2015). First and utmost, quasi-citations are characteristic of newspaper articles titles, because they are eye-catching, intriguing and evocative. They also reveal the author's assessment of the issues covered in the article. The author's wordplay and equivoque emphasizes the emotional estimative aspect of the message. It is essential for a recipient or a translator/interpreter first to recognize, identify a modified precedent unit or a quasi-citation to assess not only the meaning but also all the implications and additional emotional connotations. For instance, in the newspaper title "Wackier than thou" (The Economist, 2 January 2013) one should identify the original precedent text "holier than thou"; in the title "The Road to Hell is Paved with Bright Inventions" (The New York Times, 2 April 2005) - "The road to hell is paved with good intentions". Some witty newly coined quasi-citations can get into common usage and obtain a specific meaning. For example, "a sheep in wolf's clothing" (the original precedent unit 'a wolf in sheep's clothing') has become a catchphrase with the meaning of either someone weak and timid who behaves as a strong-willed self-assured person or something seemingly of very high quality, but in fact rather mediocre. E.g. *"Mr. Carter's closest advisers, he regards Anderson as a "fraud" - a conservative pretending to be a liberal, a sheep in wolf's clothing, who hasn't earned a place at the debating table…"* (The New York Times, 21 September 1980).

Modified historical or biblical precedent units often produce a humorous effect as in the following instance of one precedent unit, evoking certain allusions to one more precedent text, a sort of a 'matryoshka' (Russian nested doll) text. Such 'matryoshka – like' modified precedent texts are of particular interest. For instance, in the TV serial "Yes, Minister" (Great Britain 1988) one can hear the following dialogue: *"Don't look the Trojan horse into the mouth, Minister! – Why? – You can see Greeks there."* The key word combination is 'the Trojan horse'. It is used by the author in the modified saying "Don't look the gift horse into the mouth". The reference to Greeks bears allusion to one more catchphrase 'Beware of Greeks even bearing gifts'. One more associative parallel: the gift horse – gifts. In its entirety, this 'matryoshka' precedent unit produces the intended humorous effect. This is an example of both a lexical modification and a substitution of components. Apart from lexical modifications, contextual ones are not uncommon, whereby a precedent unit is used in an unusual context. For instance, *"They delivered their promise to a House committee run by John Dingell - the crusty Michigan Democrat who is another convert to the cause and has taken to describing the global warming threat with phrases like 'Hannibal is at the gates'."* (The New York Times, 13 March 2007). In this newspaper article abstract the historical catchphrase with the general meaning of warning against a serious threat occurs in the context of discussing the global warming threat - far from the historic context of the phrase. Another implication of constant repetition - pronouncing the warning repeatedly - bears association with another famous pronouncement of the same Roman senator Cato the Elder, who is said to have used the phrase "Carthage must be destroyed" as the conclusion to all his speeches.

Syntactic modifications are also not infrequent, e.g., *"The Chechen Buck Stops Where? Not in Kremlin"* (The New York Times, 29 August 1996) – modification of the catchphrase "the buck stops here" that President Truman used to express his readiness to make final decisions and take all the responsibility for them on himself. There are also cases of the author's commentary or addition: *"We mustn't throw out the baby with the bathwater of the customs union."* (The Times, 10 January 2017).

From the perspective of stylistics, precedent units can range from being elevated to humorous, even sarcastic or derisive statements. Recognizing the stylistic tinge of the discourse is one of the difficulties of comprehending and translating modified precedent units.

Misinterpreting and miscomprehension of biblical and historical catchphrases in political media discourse can evidently lead to a communication failure, as was the proverbial case with a Russian interpreter at the Nuremberg trial. When the interpreter heard the catchphrase "the Trojan horse", she started mumbling "a horse, a horse, some kind of a horse" in Russian. (Palazhchenko 1999)

Interestingly, there are instances of word-building patterns according to the productive models based on biblical or historical names, e.g., "out - Judas Judas" – "out - Napoleon Napoleon" – "out - Reagan Reagan": *It is one thing to dream of a new conservative hegemony and to thrill G.O.P. ideologues by out-Reaganing Ronald Reagan with a blizzard of anti-regulatory executive orders.* (The New York Times, 1 April 2001).

Recommendation

To sum up, it is advisable for learners of ESP and translation/interpreting skills to become conversant with the corpus of lexis under consideration, enriching the linguacultural background knowledge not only of the target, but also of the home language. The analysis of precedent units in political media discourse makes the interdisciplinary character of ESP and translation studies obvious, interface between ESP, theory of translation, theory of intercultural communication, political sciences, stylistics, history, biblical and cultural studies, to mention but a few. This convergence makes ESP and translation studies a fascinating and broadening one's horizons disciplines both to learn and to teach. In the process of learning and teaching ESP and in translation studies the importance of incorporating linguacultural awareness in the curricula thereof should not be underestimated.

References:

Bennett, M. J. 1997. How Not to Be a Fluent Fool: Understanding the Cultural Dimension of Language. In Fantini, A. E. (Ed.). New Ways in Teaching Culture Alexandria, VA: TESOL. pp. 16-21.

Byram, M. 1997. Teaching and assessing intercultural communicative competence. Clevedon: Multilingual Matters.

Kramsch, C. 1993. Context and Culture in Language Teaching. Oxford: Oxford University Press.

Leppihalme, R. 1997. Culture Bumps: An Empirical Approach to the Translation of Allusions. Topics in Translation. Clevedon: Multilingual Matters.

Los Angeles Times, 14 August 2010

Palazhchenko, P.R. 1999. My Non-Systematic Dictionary [Moy nesistematicheskij slovar]. Moscow": Valent.

Retsker, Y. I. 2007. Theory and Practice of Translation [Teorya perevoda i perevodcheskaya praktika]. Moscow: Valent.

Rubtsova, S. Y. 2005. Biblical phrases with proper names from the perspective of the difficulties of translating. Papers of VII International Philological Conference in Translation studies "Fedorovskiye chteniya". Ed, 7. Saint- Petersburg: Philological Faculty of SPb State University.

Rubtsova, S. Y. 2015. Modified precedent units with historical allusions in the English language. Difficulties of translating. Papers of XLIV International Philological Conference in Translation studies "Fedorovskiye chteniya". Ed, 24. Saint- Petersburg: Philological Faculty of SPb State University.

Safire, W. 1993. Quoth the Maven – More on Language from William Safire. New York: Random House.

The Economist, 2 January 2013

The New York Times, 2 April 2005

The New York Times, 21 September 1980

The New York Times, 13 March 2007

The New York Times, 29 August 1996

The New York Times, 1 April 2001

The Times, 10 January 2017

CHAPTER NINE

Using English-Chinese Parallel Corpus in Teaching Translation: A Study on Translator's Notes

Ting-hui Wen

Introduction

Chinese translations published in Taiwan tend to include translators' notes in various genres including mystery fiction and children's literature, such as *Harry Potter*. It is an interesting phenomenon observed in the Comparable Corpus of Chinese Mystery Fiction (CCCM), a corpus compiled to study recurrent translation features, such as simplification, explicitation, normalisation and levelling out.

The current study investigated the use of translator's notes in Chinese translations published in Taiwan with their source texts in English. For the purpose of the current study, translator's notes are defined as extra information added by the translator in the forms of footnotes, endnotes or notes inserted in the main text in parentheses. Background information added in the main texts without any parentheses are not marked and does not appear as notes for readers; therefore, it is beyond the scope of the current study.

The corpus under investigation is the Parallel Corpus of English Mystery Fiction (PCEM). The PCEM comprises eight titles of translated Chinese mystery fiction translated and published in 2005 and their source texts in English published from the years 2000 to 2005. The PCEM is an extension of the Comparable Corpus of Chinese Mystery Fiction (CCCM), which was compiled for the purpose of investigating simplification as a recurrent translation feature (Wen 2009).

In 1995, Baker first proposed using a comparable corpus to study four translation universals: simplification, explicitation, normalisation, and levelling out. A comparable corpus consists of two subcorpora, one of translated texts and the other of non-translated texts, and the two subcorpora should be in the same genre, in the same period of time and of comparable size; no source texts are included in a comparable corpus. However, a translation corpus without source texts renders mostly statistical data, and it does not show how translated texts are simplified, explicitated or normalised, or whether source texts or languages interfere with the translations.

The CCCM includes eight titles of translated mystery fiction (approximately 3229 pages) translated and published in 2005. The mystery fiction was selected as a genre under investigation due to its popularity in Taiwan, and the eight were selected based on their similar size (pages), their similar translation and publication years. It is found that seven out of eight titles of the Chinese translated mystery fiction published in Taiwan include translator's notes. The PCEM is used to study the use of translator's notes in the translations.

Literature review

Corpus-based Translation studies

In her seminal paper in 1993, Mona Baker proposed to use tools in corpus linguistics to investigate translation universals in translated texts compared with non-translated texts, which gave rise to corpus-based translation studies. The four universals, or later modified as frequent or recurrent translation patterns, are identified as simplification (Laviosa-Braithwaite 1996; Laviosa 1998, Ghadessy & Gao 2001, Wen 2009), explicitation (Olohan & Baker 2000; Chen 2004, 2006; Hu 2006), normalisation/conservatism (Kenny 1999, 2000, 2001) and levelling out. According to Baker (1996, 176-177), simplification is "the idea that translators subconsciously simplify the language or message or both"; explicitation is "the tendency to spell things out in translation, including, in its simplest form, the practice of adding background information"; normalisation or conservatism is "the tendency to conform to patterns and practices that are typical of the target language, even to the point of exaggerating them"; levelling out is "the tendency of translated texts to gravitate around the centre of any continuum rather than move towards the fringes".

Chesterman (2004, 7) labelled these universals as "descriptive universals" because they do not "incorporate ideas about what translations should or should not be, but about what translations (typically) are". Baker (1995, 234) proposed the use of a comparable corpus to investigate translation universals. A comparable corpus consists of two subcorpora, one of translated texts and the other of non-translated texts. No source texts are included in order to avoid prescriptive judgements of translation quality.

Even though some researchers have questioned representativeness of a translational corpus, saying that language is not static and samples can never be completely representative (Halverson 1998; Chesterman 2004), and that making generalisations for translations in different languages and in different times is almost impossible (Tymoczko 1998; Paloposki 2001). However, a well-designed electronic corpus enables researchers to investigate large amounts of data and compare translation universals on a large scale (Wen 2009).

At the turn of the 21st century, more projects in corpus-based translation studies have been initiated with corpora including other language pairs such as English-Norwegian (Øverås 1998 on explicitation), English-German (Schmied & Schäffler 1997 on explicitness; Steiner 2005 on explicitation), English-Finnish (Puurtinen 2004 on explicitation), German-Czech (Konšalová 2007 on explicitation), and Chinese-English (Chen 2004, 2006 on explicitation; Hu 2006 on translation universals; Wen 2009 on simplification). Research has also been conducted in the application of corpora to translator training (Zanettin 1998; Bowker 2003; Bowker and Bennison 2003; Maia 2003; Malmkjær 2003; Pearson 2003).

Translator's notes

Translator's notes are prevalent in Chinese translations published in Taiwan, including the genre in the current study, the mystery fiction. Lai (2012) mentioned that the tradition of critiques and notes of Chinese fiction is the reason why Chinese translations in the 19th century and early 20th century had notes and critiques.

The tradition continues in the 21st century. Chao (2012) studied translator's footnotes of translations of Angela Carter's novels from the sociological perspective of thick translation. She claimed that translator's notes not only help readers understand the source text, the source language, and the source culture, but can also be used to describe the influencing forces in the translating process, including the publisher, the editor and the translator.

Back in 1991, von Flowtow studied two English translations of the same French source texts and claimed that it was becoming a routine for feminist translators to "stress their active presence in the text in footnotes" (76-77).

Earlier research in translation studies seldom investigated translator's style because it was assumed that translators should be invisible and translators should faithfully transfer author's style into translated texts. However, Baker claimed that "it is impossible to produce a stretch of language in a totally impersonal way as it is to handle an object without leaving one's fingerprints on it" (2000, 244). Baker investigated the style of translation by measuring type/token ratio, measuring average sentence length and investigating reporting structures.

In addition, Baker also pointed out that translator's style might include instances of open intervention, such as "the use of prefaces or afterwords, footnotes..." (2000, 245). Translator's notes indicate the presence of translators.

Venuti disagreed with the invisibility of translators and claimed that invisibility was translators' "self-annihilation," and translation could, therefore, be marginalized (1995,8). Hermans also stated that translation had a second voice, which was the translator's voice, and the translator's note was the most overt way to present translator's voice (1996, 27). In Lai's proposal of the new translation of classic literature, she also emphasized the presence of translators, and proposed that the translator's voice should be heard (2012, 3-10).

Methodology

The PCEM comprises eight titles of English mystery fiction and their translations published in Taiwan. All the eight titles of English mystery fiction were published from the years 2001 to 2005, while their translations were all translated and published in the year 2005. The eight titles of the source texts and their translations are listed in table 1:

Table 9.1 The information of the eight titles of English mystery fiction and their translations in the PCEM

	Title	Author	Translator	Date (target texts)	Year (Source Texts)
1	*All Flowers Are Dying* 繁花將盡	Lawrence Block	You, Chuan-li (尤傳莉)	31/01/2005	2005
2	*The Twelfth Card* 第12張牌	Jeffrey Deaver	Liu, Yong-yi (劉永毅)	21/11/2005	2005
3	*3rd Degree* 第三隻魔	James Patterson	Cheng, Chia-ching (鄭家瑾)	08/03/2005	2005
4	*Monday Mourning* 泣！死神的哀悼	Kathy Reichs	Wu, Chiun-hung (吳俊宏)	28/11/2005	2004
5	*Hush* 噬血聖母的噤聲曲	Anne Frasier	Hu, Chou-hsian (胡洲賢)	01/11/2005	2002
6	*Lullaby* 搖籃曲	Chuck Palahniuk	Lu, Tsi-ying (盧慈穎)	09/10/2005	2002
7	*The Summons* 死亡傳喚	John Grisham	Song, Wei-hang (宋偉航)	01/10/2005	2002
8	*Hostage* 人質	Robert Crais	Chuang, Xu-yun (莊綉雲)	28/09/2005	2001

The current study investigated the use of translator's notes in these eight titles of translated mystery fiction. All translator's notes, which in this study is defined as extra information added by the translator in the forms of footnotes, endnotes or notes inserted in the main text between parentheses, were identified and analysed. Background information added as parts of the main text without parentheses are generally seen by the readers as part of the translation, so it is not included in this study.

Results and Data Analysis

Seven out of eight titles of translated mystery fiction in the PCEM contain translator's notes: four titles have footnotes and three have translator's notes added in the main texts between parenthesis. No endnotes are located in the PCEM. A total of 216 translator's notes are found in the PCEM, and the highest number of notes in a text is 56 (as shown in table 2)

Table 9.2 the numbers of notes and the types of notes in the PCEM

	Title	Number of pages	Number of notes	Forms of notes
1	All Flowers Are Dying	415	22	Between parentheses
2	The Twelfth Card	536	56	footnotes
3	3rd Degree	272	11	footnotes
4	Monday Mourning	400	56	footnotes
5	Hush	288	44	Between parentheses
6	Lullaby	384	53	footnotes
7	The Summons	454	19	Between parentheses
8	Hostage	480	0	

The 216 notes were further categorized into eleven types according to the information they provided: 1. information of people (n=77); 2. social and cultural information (n=40); 3. information of objects (n=33); 4. usage of languages (n=32); 5. information of organizations (21); 6. information of places; 7. allusions of literary works (n=18); 8. information of historical events (n=9); 9. information of medical terms (n=9_; 10. units of measurement (n=4); 11. the translator's interpretation (n=1). The most frequent type of notes the translators inserted in the PCEM is the information of people, and the number is 77; the least frequent type is the translator's interpretation, only one example is found in the PCEM (as shown in Table 3).

In cases when the notes could be categorized in more than one type, such as a person famous in the history, the note would be categorized based on the source text. If the source text includes only the name of the person, then the note is categorized as the information of people, instead of the information of historical events. However, if the person is fictional in a literary work, then it is categorized as allusions of literary works, instead of the information of people.

However, the translator's interpretation is a different category. The translator might add his or her own interpretations after allusions, or usages of languages, so it is categorized in both categories. Since there is only one note with the translator's interpretation, and it is categorised in both the category of allusions of literary works and the category of the translator's interpretation, the total number of notes here is 262.

Table 9.3 Types of translator's notes and their numbers

Type of notes	Number of notes
information of people	77
social and cultural information	40
information of objects	33
usage of languages	32
information of organizations	21
information of places	18
allusions of literary works	18
information of historical events	9
information of medical terms	9
units of measurement	4
the translator's interpretation	1*

Information of people

When the source text refers to a real person in the past or in the present, the translator includes the information about the person. Example 1 is a note inserted between parentheses about two names: John Alden and Priscilla Mullins. The information is about John Alden and his friend Miles Standish traveling in the ship Mayflower in 1620 to North America and his marriage to Priscilla Mullins. Example 2 is a note inserted between parentheses about Ted Bundy, a serial killer.

1. Source text:
Well, she managed to find a genealogist who was able to establish a direct line of descent from **John Alden** and **Priscilla Mullins**.

Note:
約翰．艾登（John Alden，1599-1687）與好友、鄰居邁爾斯．史坦迪許（Miles Standish）均為一六二〇年搭乘「五月花號」到達北美的英格蘭殖民者。艾登與普麗希拉．穆蘭（Priscilla Mullins）的婚姻日後成為文人筆下虛構的浪漫故事靈感來源，美國名詩人朗法羅曾有詩作（邁爾斯．史坦迪許的求婚）描寫艾登代史坦迪許向穆蘭求婚，而穆蘭卻中意艾登而結成良緣。

Back translation:
John Alden and Miles Standish, his friend and neighbour, were both English colonizers travelling to North American in Mayflowers in 1620. The marriage of Alden and Priscilla Mullins became the inspiration of fictional romantic stories for some writers. Henry Wadsworth Longfellow, a famous American poet, wrote *The Courtship of Miles Standish*, depicting how Alden proposed to Mullins on behalf of Standish, but Mullins took a liking to Alden and they got married.

2. Source text:
There had been a few cases over the years where bite marks themselves had been as incriminating as a fingerprint—Ted Bundy, for one.

Note:
泰德．邦迪（譯注：二十幾年前犯下五十件謀殺案，震驚全美的連續殺人犯，已於一九八九年元月二十四日服刑）

Back translation:
Ted Bundy (Translator's note: [he] committed 50 murders more than 20 years ago, a serial killer who shocked the whole United States of America, executed on January 24, 1989).

Social and cultural information

When the translator comes across customs or cultures existing only in the target culture, the information is included to explain the specific customs or cultures. Example 3 is a note about the parking regulations in New York, explaining why a space is good until seven the next morning. Example 4 is about Navajo dream catcher.

3. Source text:
Why go anywhere? He had **a space that was good until seven the next morning.**'

Note:
紐約因為洗街所需而有輪邊停車制度：每星期一三五街左、星期二四六街右均因為洗街而不能停車，每天早上七點換邊。

Back translation:
New York City has scheduled alternative side parking. Because of street cleaning, People are not allowed to park on the left side of the street every Monday, Wednesday and Friday, on the right side of the street every Tuesday and Thursday. The change is in effect every morning at seven o'clock.

4. Source text:
"This is **a Navajo dream catcher** I'm making," she says.

Note:
納瓦侯（Navajo）族，Navajo 的意思，是「地上的人」，他們是美國印地安居民集團中人數最多的一支，約有二十萬人，散居於新墨西哥州西北部、亞利桑那州和猶他州東南部。他們的彩陶、沙畫和毛毯遠近馳名，在納瓦侯的傳說中，住在謝依峽谷（Canyon de Chelle）蜘蛛女岩上的「蜘蛛女」（Spider Woman），傳授給納瓦侯人紡織的技藝。至今，他們還會把蜘蛛網塗在新生女嬰的手和手臂上，祈望她長大後能成為一個出色的織者。

Back translation:
Navajo, literally means people on the land, is the largest Indian American tribe, which has approximately 200,000 members. They live in the northwestern part of New Mexico, Arizona, and the southeastern part of Utah. Their pottery, sand painting and rugs are well known. In the Navajo legend, Spider Woman living on Spider Rock of Canyon de Chelle instructed the Navajo people how to weave. Nowadays, they still paint spider webs on the hands and arms of a new-born baby girl, praying for her to become an outstanding weaver after she grows up.

Information of objects

The translator includes a note of an uncommon object, such as rimfire in example 5 and Old Spice in example 6. However, rimfire was translated into Chinese, but Old Spice was not. The translator kept the source language "Old Spice" in the translation and added a footnote.

5. Source text:
He was pleased because the powerful magnum version of the **rimfire** 22-caliber bullet was rare ammunition and therefore would be easier to trace.

Note:
緣發式子彈（rimfire），一類將引藥裝在彈殼底部突出邊緣的子彈，擊錘或撞針打擊到底緣時，會引燃引藥、裝藥，進而射出子彈。

Back translation:
Rimfire ammunition is a kind of bullet that has ignition inserted at the base's rim. When the firing pin strikes the rim, it will ignite the primer and the bullet will be discharged.

6. Source text: Cyr shuffled to the recliner and lowered himself, a tsunami of **Old Spice** following in his wake.

Note:
一種便宜的古龍水。

Back translation:
A cheap cologne.

Usage of languages

In case of puns or the usage of another language in the source text, the translator tries to explain the usage of language in the notes. Example 7 explains a pun and an allusion to the Bible. In example 8, the translator kept the French word *demimonde* in the translation and added a note to explain this French word.

7. Source text:
We are living in **the tower of babble**. (Lullaby)

Note: 現今時常使用的一種說法，babble是嬰兒牙牙學語的意思，引申為說話不清不楚。這個說法是緣起於嬰兒學語或者Tower of Babel聖經中蓋在巴比倫城的巴別塔，人類想要蓋一座高塔通上天堂，卻激怒了上帝，上帝因而使人類說起不同的語言，彼此無法溝通，因而無法完成高塔。

Back translation:
It is a common expression nowadays. Babble means babies talking unintelligibly, and it can be used to describe people talking in an incomprehensible way.
According to the Bible, the Tower of Babel was built in the city of Babylon. People there planned to build a tower to reach heaven, and this plan angered God. God made people speak different languages, so they could not communicate with one another and could not finish the tower.

8. Source text:
They are, I suppose, of the underworld, though Elaine thinks the French word **demimonde** is more suitable, if only because it's French.

Note:
demimonde源於法文，指富人包養或保護的女性族群，或是妓女族群、邊緣族群。

Back translation:
demimonde, originated from French, refers to a group of women with a steady income and protection from their rich lovers, or a group of prostitutes or a marginal group.

Information of organizations

Information of companies or organizations is sometimes added by the translator as well. The translation of example 9 does not include the source language HMO, but it has a note explaining the abbreviation of HMO. Example 10 includes the shop name in English without Chinese translation, but a note is added to explain Anthropologie.

9. Source text:
[H]e had no flair for urology and found his true calling stringing together failing regional insurers into giant **HMOs**.

Note: 大型健保公司，原文為HMO，Health Maintenance Organization，美國醫療保險體系的一種。

Back translation:
A big insurance group. Health Maintenance Organization, HMO, is part of the American insurance system.

10. Source text:
I especially crave that sweater from **Anthropologie**.

Note:
美國一間販售衣物家飾的零售商

Back translation:
An American retailer selling clothing, home furniture and décor.

Information of places

Information of places, cities or countries is added as notes by the translator. Example 11 gives the information of Cardiff. Example 12 clarifies that Oxford here refers to a city in the United States, not the city in England.

11. Source text:
I don't think this guy's from Cardiff.

Note:
卡地夫(Cardiff)是英國威爾斯的首府。

Back translation:
Cardiff is the capital of Wales in the United Kingdom.

12. Source text:
That was that Chadwick fella over in **Oxford**, wasn't it?" French said smugly, and Ray was speechless.

Note: 此處的牛津是位於密西西比州。

Back translation:
Oxford here is located in Mississippi.

Allusions of literary works

When the source text includes allusions to literary works in the source language, the translator might consider it necessary to give the readers information. Example 13 gives information of George Orwell's *Nineteen Eighty-Four* and who or what Big Brother refers to. The translator of examples 14 and 15 gave the references for two of the quotes but did not explain further why the characters in *Morning Mourning* quoted *Mother Goose* and *Hamlet*.

13. Source text:
Old George Orwell got it backward. Big Brother isn't watching.

Note:
老大哥指的是喬治．歐威爾 (1903-1950) 的諷刺寓言小說《一九八四》中無所不在的監視系統。

Back translation:
Big Brother refers to the ubiquitous surveillance in George Orwell's (1903-1960) satire *Nineteen Eighty-Four*.

14. Source text:
"All the king's horses and all the king's men can't put the damned back together again." Singsong.

Note:
這首 Humpty Dumpty 是鵝媽媽童謠裡面的一首兒歌。

Back translation:
"Humpty Dumpty" is a nursery rhyme in *Mother Goose*.

15. Source text:
"Did she actually do the 'get thee to a nunnery' bit?"

Note:
get thee to a nunnery 為莎劇『哈姆雷特』中的一句台詞。

Back translation:
"get thee to a nunnery" is a line in Shakespeare's *Hamlet*.

Information of historical events

When the source text mentions historical events, the translator adds background information of these events. In Example 16, four footnotes are inserted at the bottom of the page, one of the information of people, and three of the information of historical events.

16. Source text:
"We've heard it all over and over.... Amistad, slavers, John Brown, the Jim Crow laws, Brown versus the Board of Education, Martin Luther King, Jr., Malcolm X..."

Note 1:
亞美士達 (Amistad) 事件』是美國黑奴史上一個極為重要的事件：一群黑奴在亞美士達號奴隸船上為爭取自由而進行『叛變』，殺掉了奴隸販子，結果在美國最高法院獲判無罪。

Back translation 1:
Amistad is an important event in the American history of slavery. A group of African slaves started a revolt on the ship La Amistad, killing the human trafficker. The supreme court ruled them innocent and ordered them freed.

Note 2:
美國南北內戰結束後，南方各州政府所制訂的黑白『平等但隔離』法律，表面上平等，實則歧視黑人，後來在民權運動風起雲湧後遭廢除。

Back translation2:
After American Civil War, the State governments in the South enforced racial segregation laws, which appeared to be equal but in fact discriminating. The laws were abolished after the Civil Rights Movement.

Note 3:
美國堪薩斯州皮托卡市的琳達．布朗一直被拒於該街區的白人學校之外，於是對學校的種族隔離政策提出法律告訴。一九五四年五月十七日，美國最高法院全體一致作出裁決：公立學校的種族隔離違反憲法。此一裁決為黑人民權運動史上的里程碑。

Back translation 3:
Linda Brown in Topeka Kansa was rejected to be enrolled at an all-white school in her block, so her family filed a lawsuit against the racial segregation of the schools. On May 17 1954, the Supreme Court ruled that racial segregation in public schools violated the constitution. The ruling is a milestone in Civil Rights Movement.

Information of medical terms

In the genre of mystery fiction, medical terms might show up in forensic scenes. The translator included notes to explain these terms. In example 17, the translator of *Hush* inserted the note of DQA1 between parentheses. Example 18 is about a drug.

17. Source text:
"Unfortunately, The DQA1 involves minute amounts of secretions, and there are very few lab technicians trained to run these tests.

Note:
DQA1測試 (譯注：基因鑑定系統的鹼基多型，也就是更精密的DNA測試)

Back translation:
DQA1 tests (Translator's note: The HLA-DQA1 gene is part of a family of genes called the human leukocyte antigen (HLA) complex. A DQA1 test is a more precise DNA test).

18. Source text:
"That is the Ambien that was sent to us?" LaManche asked.

Note:
一種法國藥廠所生產的安眠藥。

Back translation:
A kind of sleeping pills produced by a French pharmaceutical company.

Unit of measurement

The metric system is adopted in Taiwan. When the translator encounters the imperial system in the source text, he or she either changes the unit of measurement directly into the metric system, or they keeps the original system and adds a note (see example 19).

19. Source text:
He picked up a quart jar of spaghetti sauce.

Note:
一夸爾 (譯注：約零點九五公升)

Back translation:
A quart (translator's note: approximately 0.95 liter).

The translator's interpretation

Only one note out of the total 261 translator's notes found in the PCEM is the translator's interpretation of the source text. In example 20, the translator explained what Neverland and Oz are first, and then continued to tell the readers that the character Rhyme was just being cynical.

20. Source text:
Where would that particular hospital be, Thom? Neverland? Oz?

Note:
夢幻島 (Neverland) 是小飛俠彼得潘的家，翡翠城 (Oz) 是《綠野仙蹤》(The Wizard of Oz) 中奧茲大王居住的城堡，兩者均是童話中的美好虛幻之地，萊姆只是一貫的譏誚。

Back translation:
Neverland is the home of Peter Pan, and Oz is the castle that the ruler of the Land of Oz resides in *The Wizard of Oz*. Both places are fictitious. Rhyme was just being cynical as usual.

Conclusion and further research

In Chinese translations, adding notes is a frequent phenomenon. Translators might try to give information about people, places, historical events, social phenomenon of the source culture, and allusions of the literary works. Moreover, notes might solve the problems of translatability, especially when the source text has puns which cannot be translated. Among the eleven types of notes found in the PCEM, the translator's personal interpretation of the source text is the most obvious intervention.

Translator's notes can also be a manifestation of explicitation. According to Baker (1996, 177) explicitation is "the tendency to spell things out in translation, including, in its simplest form, the practice of adding background information."

Translator's notes can be seen as either a distraction or an assistance for the readers. In teaching translation, there might be controversies regarding how many notes and what kind of notes to be inserted in translations. Further research on the reader's reception might help solve the disputes.

References

Baker, M. 1995. "Corpora in translation studies: An overview and some suggestions for future research", *Target* 7 (2): 223-243.

Baker, M. 1996. "Corpus-based translation studies: The challenges that lie ahead" in H. Somers (ed.) *Terminology, LSP and Translation Studies in Language Engineering: In honour of Juan C. Sager*, Amsterdam and Philadelphia: John Benjamins, pp. 175-186.

Baker, M. 2000. "Toward a methodology for investigating the style of a literary translator," *Target* 12 (2): 241-266.

Bowker, L. 2003. "Corpus-based applications for translator training: Exploring the possibilities", in S. Granger, J. Lerot and S. Petch-Tyson (eds.) *Corpus-based Approaches to Contrastive Linguistics and Translation Studies*, Amsterdam and New York: Rodopi, pp. 169-184.

Bowker, L., Bennison, P. 2003. "Student translation archive and student translation tracking system design, development and application" in F. Zanettin, S. Bernardini and D. Stewart (eds.) *Corpora in Translator Education*, Manchester: St. Jerome Publishing, pp. 103-118.

Chao, J. 2012. "Thick Translation" as an approach to translational footnotes: Angela Carter's fiction in Taiwan," *Studies of Translation and Interpretation* 15: 19-40.

Chen, J. W. (2004) "Investigating explicitation of conjunctions in translated Chinese: A corpus-based study," *Language Matters* 35 (1): 295-312.

Chen, J. W. 2006. *Explicitation Through the Use of Connectives in Translated Chinese: A corpus-based study*, Unpublished PhD thesis, The University of Manchester.

Chesterman, A. 2004. "Beyond the particular", in Anna Mauranen and Pekka Kujamäki (eds.), *Translation Universals: Do they exist?*, Amsterdam & Philadelphia: John Benjamins, pp. 33-50.

Ghadessy, M., Gao, Y. 2001. "Simplification as a universal feature of the language of translation", *Journal of Asian Pacific Communication* 11 (1):61-75.

Halverson, S. 1998. "Translation studies and representative corpora: Establishing links between translation corpora, theoretical/descriptive categories and a conception of the object of study", *Meta* 43 (4): 494-514.

Hermans, T. 1996. "The translator's voice in translated narrative", *Target* 8 (1): 23-48.

Hu, X. 2006. *A Corpus-based Study on the Translation Norms of Contemporary Chinese Translated Fiction*, unpublished PhD thesis, East China Normal University.

Kenny, D. 1999. *Norms and Creativity: Lexis in translated text* unpublished PhD thesis, UMIST.

Kenny, D. 2000. "Lexical hide-and-seek: Looking for creativity in a parallel corpus" in Maeve Olohan (ed.) *Intercultural Faultlines: Research models in translation studies I: textual and cognitive aspects*, Manchester: St. Jerome Publishing, pp. 93-104.

Kenny, D. 2001. *Lexis and Creativity in Translation: A corpus-based study*, Manchester: St. Jerome Publishing.

Konšalová, P. 2007. "Explicitation as a universal in syntactic de/condensation", *Across Languages and Cultures* 8 (1): 17-32.

Lai, S. T. 2012. "Translator as commentator: On the Translator's Notes by Woo Kuang Kien", *Compilation and Translation Review* 5 (2): 1-29.

Laviosa-Braithwaite, S. 1996. *The English Comparable Corpus(ECC): a resource and a methodology for the empirical study of translation*, Unpublished PhD thesis, UMIST.

Laviosa-Braithwaite, S. 1998. "Core patterns of lexical use in a comparable corpus of English narrative prose", *Meta* 43 (4): 557-570.

Maia, B. 2003. "Training translators in terminology and information retrieval using comparable and parallel corpora", in Federico Zanettin, Silvia Bernardini and Dominic Stewart (eds.) *Corpora in Translator Education*, Manchester, St. Jerome Publishing, pp. 43-54.

Malmkjær, K. 2003. "On a pseudo-subversive use of corpora in translator training", in Federico Zanettin, Silvia Bernardini and Dominic Stewart (eds.) *Corpora in Translator Education*, Manchester, St. Jerome Publishing, pp. 119-134.

Olohan, M., Baker, M. 2000. "Reporting that in translated English. Evidence for subconscious processes of explicitation?", *Across Languages and Cultures* 1 (2): 141-158.

Øverås, L. 1998. "In search of the third code: an investigation of norms in literary translation," *Meta: Translators' Journal* 43 (4): 571-588.

Paloposki, O. 2001. "Enriching translations, simplified language? An alternative viewpoint to lexical simplification", *Target* 13 (2): 265-288.

Pearson, J. 2003. "Using parallel texts in the translator training environment" in F. Zanettin, S. Bernardini and D. Stewart (eds.) *Corpora in Translator Education*, Manchester: St. Jerome Publishing, pp. 15-24.

Puurtinen, T. 2003. "Genre-specific features of translationese? Linguistic differences between translated and non-translated Finnish children's literature", *Literary and Linguistic Computing* 18 (4): 389-406.

Schmied, J., Schäffler, H. 1997. "Explicitness as a universal feature of translation", in Magnus Ljung (ed.), Corpus-based Studies in English: Papers from the Seventeenth International Conference on English Language Research on Computerized Corpora, Amsterdam and Atlanta: Rodopi, pp. 21-34.

Steiner, E. 2005. "Explicitation, its lexicogrammatical realization, and its determining (independent) variables—towards an empirical and corpus-based methodology" SPRIKreports 36:1-43.

Tymoczko, M. 1998. "Computerized corpora and translation studies", *Meta* 43 (4), 652-659.

Venuti, A. 1995. *The Translator's Invisibility: A History of Translation*, New York and London: Routledge.

von Flotow, L. 1991. "Feminist translation: Contexts, practices and theories", *TTR: traduction, terminologie, redaction* 4(2): 69-84.

Wen, T. 2009. *Simplification as a Recurrent Translation Feature: A corpus-based study of modern Chinese translated mystery fiction in Taiwan*, unpublished PhD thesis, University of Manchester.

Zanettin, F. 1998. "Bilingual comparable corpora and the training of translators", *Meta* 43 (4): 616-630.

CHAPTER TEN

Motivation in Teaching Speaking in ESP: A Comparison between Two Private Lebanese Universities

Wassim Bekai, Samar Harkouss

Introduction

In learning any language, speaking plays an essential part in language acquisition. This has been a problematic issue as language teachers aspire to improve students' communicative skills through the use of different techniques such as role play, discussions, simulations among others or by improving students' vocabulary and pronunciation. The study sheds light on the importance of intrinsic and extrinsic motivation in an English speaking class where English is taught as a foreign language for specific purposes such as business English, aviation English training among others, and whether motivation is linked to academic, linguistic and socio-cultural factors. The importance of developing speaking skills in these specific situations has a great impact on students' academic, social and professional development. The aim of the study was to investigate the similarities and differences between The University of Balamand (hereafter UoB) 72 students where the UoB is in the northern part of Lebanon and The American University of Beirut (hereafter AUB) 50 students where AUB is in the capital Beirut. The participants were diverse, majored in different fields and were divided between sophomore, junior and senior students on the one hand and the students' gender on the other. The reason behind this division was to test both intrinsic and extrinsic motivation and which group is more motivated. SPSS statistical analyses show a variation in the results between the two groups. The test revealed that there are differences between the two groups of students when it comes to motivation and its relation to academic, linguistic and sociocultural factors.

The teaching of English as a foreign language in Lebanese universities has typically focused on teaching grammar, vocabulary, reading, and writing and marginalized speaking. In learning any language, speaking plays an essential part in language acquisition. The academic, linguistic and socio-cultural factors play an important role in students' competence and performance when it comes to speaking. According to Light, Cox, and Calkins (2009), teaching is not helping students' memorizing and accumulating separate words from language books; it is how to perform, how to put the words together to form sentences and be able to participate in a conversation. Banks and McGee-Banks (2009) explain that in multicultural educational institutions changing the teaching and learning techniques helps students of both genders in diverse cultural, ethnic and language groups to have equal opportunities to learn.

Research Questions

The study aimed to investigate and study the impact of motivation on students' speaking skills and how it influences UoB and AUB students' academic, social and professional development; and to explore the relationship between motivation and academic, linguistic and socio-cultural factors and their effect on speaking skills.

Methodology

The study investigated the UoB 72 and AUB 50 diverse participants from different majors who were divided between sophomore, junior and senior students on the one hand and the students' gender on the other. The reason behind this division was to test both intrinsic and extrinsic motivation and which group is more motivated. Data was collected by asking students to fill closed-ended questionnaires and SPSS statistical analyses showed a variation in the results between the two groups and this is due to a variety of factors. This study followed an exploratory approach and aimed to collect data on students' perceptions of the importance of speaking skills and the reasons behind their motivation or lack of motivation. Ethical issues were taken into consideration where students agreed to participate in this study.

Literature Review

In the English classroom many skills are taught. One of these skills is speaking. Shumin (1997) states that learning how to speak a second language, in this case, English, is not only about knowing the grammatical rules of a language, but it is also about knowing how to communicate with native-like accuracy outside the four walls of the classroom. Luoma (2004) believes that speaking is a social activity that is used to show a person's personality, thoughts, and his/her ability to express themselves to others. She states that it is an essential skill to communicate with others in different social contexts. Therefore, learners improve their speaking skills by sharing ideas, discussing information, negotiating meaning, and understanding what is spoken to them in different circumstances. (Anton 1999).

Speaking

The students' communicative skills are today's goal of teaching speaking. A speaking skill in class is given importance by Baker and Westrup (2003) who state that a classroom is a place where students can practice using the language in a supportive environment and not only a place where they learn about the rules of language. The success in language learning and the effectiveness of the English course are evaluated by learners according to how well they feel they have improved in their spoken language proficiency.

Speaking anxiety

Lake and Pappamihiel (2003) clarify the complexity of the anxiety concept which depends upon not only one's feelings of self-efficacy but also appraisals regarding the potential and perceived threats inherent in certain situations. Horwitz, Horwitz, and Cope (1986, 132) pointed out that "since speaking in the target language seems to be the most threatening aspect of foreign language learning, the current emphasis on the development of communicative competence poses particularly great difficulties for the anxious student". Horwitz, Horwitz, and Cope (1986) argue that most people when learning a new language feel reduced to a childlike state when asked to use their second language. They add that learners of a foreign language are often subjected to threats to their self-perception in the foreign language classroom setting.

Motivation

Definition

Deci & Ryan (2000) explain the term motivation as the feeling of a person who is energised or activated towards an end, thus to be motivated means to be moved to do something. The authors clarify that people vary in the type of motivation (orientation) and not only in the amount of motivation (level of motivation).

Types of motivation

When motivation is discussed, a distinction is made between amotivation, extrinsic and intrinsic motivation. (Harmer 2001). Amotivation happens when a person has very low levels of motivation towards any given task. Extrinsic motivation, on the other hand, is external where students are motivated because of external factors such as passing an exam, applying for jobs etc...

By intrinsic motivation, students are motivated for self-fulfilment purposes, it is an internal feeling and they want to feel satisfied.

Motivation to learn

In defining 'Motivation to learn' Brophy (1983) explained its general trait and its situational-specific state. The author elaborates that motivation to learn, as a general trait, refers to an enduring disposition to value, learning for its own sake- to enjoy the process and take pride in the outcomes of experiences involving knowledge acquisition or skill development. In the specific situation, the writer says that a state of motivation to learn exists when students engage themselves purposively in classroom tasks by trying to master the concepts or skills involved.

Lack of effort/motivation

Deci and Ryan (2000) explain the term amotivation as the relative absence of motivation that is caused by the individual's experiencing feelings of incompetence and helplessness when faced with activity and not by a lack of initial interest. Another definition of lack of motivation was given by Dornyei (2005, 143) who explains it as "specific external forces that reduce or diminish the motivational basis of a behavioural intention or an ongoing action".

Demotives

Dornyei (2005) listed reasons for a learner to lose his/her interest in class which he called demotives. The author explains that demotives are the negative counterparts of motives; and whereas motives increase action tendency, demotives de-energize it. Gorham and Christophel (1992) summarised the rank of order of the fluency of the various demotives, with first five categories as dissatisfaction with grading and assignments; the teacher being boring, bored, unorganized and unprepared; the dislike of the subject area; the inferior organization of the teaching material and the teacher being unapproachable, self-centered, biased, condescending and insulting.

Preliminary Analyses

Preliminary analyses were examined before conducting the main data analysis. The preliminary analysis involved missing value analysis, reliability analysis and analysis of univariate and multivariate outliers.

Missing value analysis

The missing value analysis revealed that all the variables had less than 5% of missing values except for gender (21.3%), item number 7 (8.2%) of the academic factors scale and item number 4 (9.8%) of the socio-cultural factors scale. The Little's MCAR test was conducted to test whether the data was missing completely at random or not. The results of the Little's MCAR test was statistically significant indicating that MCAR (missing completely at random) cannot be inferred; X^2 (1744) = 1858.05, p = .029. To test whether the missing data has any impact on the main analysis, three independent t-tests were run. The variable (gender) that had missing values above 5% was recoded. The ranges of acceptable values were coded into 1 and the missing values were coded into 2. These two groups were compared on the outcome variables (academic, linguistic and socio-cultural factors) using three independent t-tests. The results revealed that there were no significant differences on the outcome variables (academic and socio-cultural factors) between participants who had left missing data and those who had not left missing data on gender. The results, revealed, however, that participants who had left missing data had significantly lower levels of linguistic factors compared to participants who had not left missing data on gender.

Reliability analysis

The reliability analysis revealed that all the scales were reliable. Precisely, the two scales, intrinsic motivation and linguistic factors had very good reliability with α = .87 and α = .85 respectively. The two scales, extrinsic motivation and amotivation had good reliability with α = .76 and α = .79 respectively. Finally, the two scales, academic and socio-cultural factors had acceptable reliability with α = .68 and α = .55 respectively (see Table 1).

Table 10.1
Reliability of the Scales: Cronbach's alpha

Scales and Subscales	Cronbach's alpha	N of items
Intrinsic motivation	.87	12
Extrinsic motivation	.76	12
Amotivation	.79	4
Academic factors	.68	11
Linguistic factors	.85	8
Socio-cultural factors	.55	9

Univariate and multivariate outliers

Univariate outliers were inspected using z-scores. Any case with z-score above ± 3.00 standard deviations is considered as a univariate outlier. The results revealed that there were two univariate outliers with z-scores above ±3.00 standard deviations on the predictor variable intrinsic motivation with case # 19 and 22, one univariate outlier on the predictor variable extrinsic motivation with case # 22 and one univariate outlier on the predictor variable amotivation with case # 72. The results revealed, however, that there were no univariate outliers on the outcome variables (academic, linguistic and socio-cultural factors). Multivariate outliers were inspected through Mahalanobis distances. No cases were found to be multivariate outliers, $\chi2\ (3) = 17.88$, $p < .001$, (critical value = 18.47). Since the univariate outliers (case # 19, 22 and 72) were not found to be multivariate outliers, they were retained in the final data analysis.

Sample Characteristics

The final sample of the study was composed of $N = 122$ participants with $N = 50$ (41%) from The American University of Beirut (AUB) university and $N = 72$ (59%) from The University of Balamand (UoB). (See figure 1). The sample was composed of equal percentage of males (49%) and females (51%). The means and standard deviations of the scales are presented in Table 2. On average, participants had high levels of intrinsic motivation ($M = 3.60$, $SD = 0.63$) and extrinsic motivation ($M = 4.04$, $SD = 0.50$). Participants, however, on average had low levels of amotivation ($M = 1.83$, $SD = 0.95$). Finally, on average, participants had high levels of academic ($M = 3.80$, $SD = 0.56$), linguistic ($M = 3.25$, $SD = 0.83$) and socio-cultural factors ($M = 3.57$, $SD = 0.53$).

Fig. 10.1.

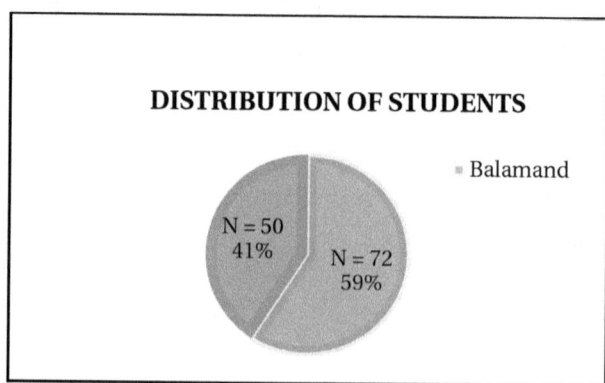

Table 10.2
Scale descriptive

	N	Minimum	Maximum	Mean	Std. Deviation
Intrinsic	122	1.42	5.00	3.60	.63
Extrinsic	122	2.42	5.00	4.04	.50
Amotivation	122	1.00	5.00	1.83	.95
Academic factors	122	2.55	4.91	3.80	.56
Linguistic factors	122	1.00	4.88	3.25	.83
Socio-culural factors	119	2.25	5.00	3.57	.53
Valid N (listwise)	119				

Correlation between Predictors and Outcome Variables

Normality analysis

a- UoB sample

The normality of variables was tested by examining the z-scores of skewness and kurtosis. The normality analysis revealed that the predictor variable (extrinsic motivation) and the outcome variables (academic, linguistic and socio-cultural factors) had z-skewness scores and z-kurtosis scores below the ±1.96 significance level, indicating that these variables were normally distributed. The normality analysis, however, revealed that the predictor variables (intrinsic and amotivation) had z-skewness scores and z-kurtosis scores above the ±1.96 significance level, indicating that these variables were not normally distributed. Since the normality of the predictor variable extrinsic motivation was met, then a Pearson test was conducted to study the relation between extrinsic motivation and the outcome variables; academic, linguistic and socio-cultural factors (see Table 3). However, since normality of the predictor variables intrinsic motivation and amotivation was not met, then Spearman Rho's tests were conducted to study the relation between the predictor intrinsic motivation and amotivation and the outcome variables academic, linguistic and socio-cultural factors (see Table 4).

b- AUB sample

The normality of variables was tested by examining the z-scores of skewness and kurtosis. The normality analysis revealed that the predictor variable (intrinsic motivation) and the outcome variables (academic, linguistic and socio-cultural factors) had z-skewness scores and z-kurtosis scores below the

±1.96 significance level, indicating that these variables were normally distributed. The normality analysis, however, revealed that the predictor variables (extrinsic and amotivation) had z-skewness scores and z-kurtosis scores above the ±1.96 significance level, indicating that these variables were not normally distributed. Since the normality of the predictor variable intrinsic motivation was met, then a Pearson test was conducted to study the relation between intrinsic motivation and the outcome variables; academic, linguistic and socio-cultural factors (see Table 5). However, since normality of the predictor variables extrinsic motivation and amotivation was not met, then Spearman Rho's tests were conducted to study the relation between the predictors extrinsic motivation and amotivation and the outcome variables academic, linguistic and socio-cultural factors (see Table 6).

Correlation between extrinsic, intrinsic and amotivation and academic factors

a- UoB Sample

The Pearson Correlation test revealed that there was a significant positive and medium correlation between extrinsic motivation and academic factors; $r = .29$, $p = .006$ (one-tailed); indicating that participants who had higher levels of extrinsic motivation tended to have higher levels of academic factors. In addition, the Spearman Rho's correlation test revealed that there was a significant positive and medium to large correlation between intrinsic motivation and academic factors; $r_s = .38$, $p = .001$ (one-tailed); indicating that participants who had higher levels of intrinsic motivation tended to have higher levels of academic factors. Finally, the Spearman Rho's correlation test revealed that there was a significant negative and medium to large correlation between amotivation and academic factors; $r_s = -.42$, $p < .001$ (one-tailed); indicating that participants who had higher levels of amotivation tended to have lower levels of academic factors.

b- AUB sample

The Spearman Rho's correlation test revealed that there was a significant positive and medium to large correlation between extrinsic motivation and academic factors; $r_s = .41$, $p = .002$ (one-tailed); indicating that participants who had higher levels of extrinsic motivation tended to have higher levels of academic factors. The Pearson correlation test also revealed that there was a significant positive and large correlation between intrinsic motivation and academic factors $r = .50$, $p < .001$ (one-tailed); indicating that participants who had higher levels of intrinsic motivation tended to have higher levels of academic factors. Finally, the Spearman Rho's correlation test revealed that there was no significant correlation between amotivation and academic factors; $r_s = .06$, $p = .34$, ns (one-tailed).

Correlation between extrinsic, intrinsic and amotivation and linguistic factors

a- UoB sample

The Pearson Correlation test revealed that there was no significant relation between extrinsic motivation and linguistic factors; $r = .03$, $p = .41$, ns (one-tailed). Similarly, the Spearman Rho's correlation test revealed that there was no significant relation between intrinsic motivation and the linguistic factors; $r_s = -.04$, $p = .37$, ns (one-tailed). Finally, the Spearman Rho's correlation test revealed that there was a significant negative and medium to large correlation between amotivation and the linguistic factors; $r_s = -.43$, $p < .001$ (one-tailed); indicating that participants who had higher levels of amotivation tended to have lower levels of linguistic factors.

b- AUB sample

The Spearman's rho Correlation test revealed that there was no significant relation between extrinsic motivation and linguistic factors; $r_s = -.06$, $p = .34$, ns (one-tailed). Similarly, the Pearson correlation test revealed that there was no significant relation between intrinsic motivation and the linguistic factors; $r = .01$, $p = .48$, ns (one-tailed). Finally, the Spearman Rho's correlation test revealed that there was a significant negative and medium to large correlation between amotivation and the linguistic factors; $r_s = -.31$, $p = .014$ (one-tailed); indicating that participants who had higher levels of amotivation tended to have lower levels of linguistic factors.

Correlation between extrinsic, intrinsic and amotivation and socio-cultural factors

a- UoB sample

The Pearson Correlation test revealed that there was a significant positive and medium to large correlation between extrinsic motivation and socio-cultural factors; $r = .33$, $p = .003$ (one-tailed); indicating that participants who had higher levels of extrinsic motivation tended to have higher levels of socio-cultural factors. In addition, the Spearman Rho's correlation test revealed that there was a significant positive and medium to large correlation between intrinsic motivation and socio-cultural factors; $r_s = .35$, $p = .001$ (one-tailed); indicating that participants who had higher levels of intrinsic motivation tended to have higher levels of socio-cultural factors. Finally, the Spearman Rho's correlation test revealed that there was a significant negative and medium to large correlation between amotivation and socio-cultural factors; $r_s = -.38$, $p = .001$ (*one-tailed*); indicating that participants who had higher levels of amotivation tended to have lower levels of socio-cultural factors.

b- AUB sample

The Spearman rho's Correlation test revealed that there was a significant positive and medium to large correlation between extrinsic motivation and socio-cultural factors; $r_s = .37$, $p = .004$ (*one-tailed*); indicating that participants who had higher levels of extrinsic motivation tended to have higher levels of socio-cultural factors. In addition the Pearson correlation test revealed that there was no significant correlation between intrinsic motivation and socio-cultural factors; $r = .23$, $p = .06$, *ns* (*one-tailed*). Finally, the Spearman Rho's correlation test revealed that there was a non-significant correlation between amotivation and socio-cultural factors; $r_s = -.06$, p

Table 10.3
UoB Sample: Pearson Zero Order Correlation Matrix

	Academic factors	Linguistic factors	Socio-cultural factors
Extrinsic motivation	.29**	.03	.33**

Table 10.4
Blamand Sample: Spearman Rho's Zero Order Correlation Matrix

	Academic factors	Linguistic factors	Socio-cultural factors
Intrinsic motivation	.38**	-.04	.35**
Amotivation	-.42***	-.43**	-.38**

**. Correlation is significant at the 0.01 level (one-tailed).
***. Correlation is significant at the 0.001 level (one-tailed).

Table 10.5
AUB Sample: Pearson Zero Order Correlation Matrix

	Academic factors	Linguistic factors	Socio-cultural factors
Intrinsic motivation	.50***	.01	.23

***. Correlation is significant at the 0.001 level (one-tailed).

Table 10.6
AUB Sample: Spearman Rho's Zero Order Correlation Matrix

	Academic factors	Linguistic factors	Socio-cultural factors
Extrinsic motivation	.41**	-.06	.37**
Amotivation	.06	-.31*	-.06

*. Correlation is significant at the 0.05 level (one-tailed).
**. Correlation is significant at the 0.01 level (one-tailed).

Regression analysis: predictors of academic factors

a- UoB sample

The F-test revealed that the regression model which contained the predictors (intrinsic, extrinsic and amotivation) was significantly better than the mean in explaining the variance in the outcome variable (academic factors), $F(3, 68) = 10.11$, $p < .001$. Moreover, the regression model which contained those predictors explained 30.8% ($R^2 = .308$) of the variance of the outcome variable (academic factors) at the sample level. The adjusted R square for the regression model was $R^2 adj = .278$, indicating that this regression model explained 27.8% of the variance of the outcome variable (academic factors) at the level of the population. In addition, when moving from the sample to the population, the shrinkage $\Delta R^2 = 3.0\%$; indicating that the sample is a good representation of the population (see Table 7). By inspecting the table of coefficients, the t-test revealed that out of the three predictors, extrinsic motivation and amotivation were significant predictors of academic factors with amotivation being the highest predictor. Precisely, the t-test revealed that amotivation was a significant negative and medium to large predictor of academic factors; $b = -.22$, $\beta = -.41$, $t(68) = -4.08$, $p < .001$. This indicates that participants who had higher levels of amotivation tended to have lower levels of academic factors. The t-test also revealed that intrinsic motivation was a significant positive and medium predictor of academic factors; $b = .24$, $\beta = .29$, $t(68) = 2.57$, $p = .012$. This indicates that participants who had higher levels of intrinsic motivation tended to have higher levels of academic factors. However, there was no relation between extrinsic motivation and academic factors. (see Table 8).

Table 10.7
R, R Square, Adjusted R Square

Model	R	R Square	Adjusted R Square	Std. Error of the Estimate	R Square Change	F Change	df1	df2	Sig. F Change	Durbin-Watson
1	.56	.308	.278	.48	.31	10.11	3	68	.000	1.65

Table 10.8
Regression Parameters

Model		B	SE B	β
1	(Constant)	2.62	.46	
	Intrinsic motivation	.24	.09	.29*
	Extrinsic motivation	.15	.12	.14
	Amotivation	-.22	.05	-.41***

Note: For model 1; $R^2 = .31$, $\Delta R^2 = .03$, * $p < .05$, ** $p < .01$, *** $p < .001$

b- AUB sample

The F-test revealed that the regression model which contained the predictors (intrinsic, extrinsic and amotivation) was significantly better than the mean in explaining the variance in the outcome variable (academic factors), $F(3, 46) = 5.85$, $p = .002$. Moreover, the regression model which contained those predictors explained 27.6% ($R^2 = .276$) of the variance of the outcome variable (academic factors) at the sample level. The adjusted R square for the regression model was $R^2adj = .229$, indicating that this regression model explained 22.9% of the variance of the outcome variable (academic factors) at the level of the population. In addition, when moving from the sample to the population, the shrinkage $\Delta R^2 = 4.7\%$; indicating that the sample is a good representation of the population (see Table 9). By inspecting the table of coefficients, the t-test revealed that out of the three predictors, extrinsic motivation was the only significant predictor of academic factors. Precisely, the t-test revealed that intrinsic motivation was a significant positive and medium to large predictor of academic factors; $b = .39$, $β = .42$, $t(46) = 3.00$, $p = .004$. This indicates that participants who had higher levels of intrinsic motivation tended to have higher levels of academic factors. However, there was no relation between the predictors (extrinsic motivation and amotivation) and academic factors. (see Table 10).

Table 10.9
R, R Square, Adjusted R Square

Model	R	R Square	Adjusted R Square	Std. Error of the Estimate	Change Statistics					Durbin-Watson
					R Square Change	F Change	df1	df2	Sig. F Change	
1	.53	.276	.229	.38	.28	5.85	3	46	.002	2.81

Table 10.10
Regression Parameters

Model		B	SE B	β
1	(Constant)	1.81	.58	
	Intrinsic motivation	.39	.13	.42**
	Extrinsic motivation	.19	.14	.19
	Amotivation	-.01	.09	-.01

Note: For model 1; $R^2 = .276$, $\Delta R^2 = .047$, ** $p < .01$,

Regression analysis: predictors of linguistic factors

a- UoB sample

The F-test revealed that the regression model which contained the predictors (intrinsic, extrinsic and amotivation) was significantly better than the mean in explaining the variance in the outcome variable (linguistic factors), F (3, 68) = 7.15, $p < .001$. Moreover, the regression model which contained those predictors explained 24% ($R^2 = .24$) of the variance of the outcome variable (linguistic factors) at the sample level. The adjusted R square for the regression model was $R^2 adj = .206$, indicating that this regression model explained 20.6% of the variance of the outcome variable (linguistic factors) at the level of the population. In addition, when moving from the sample to the population, the shrinkage $\Delta R^2 = 3.4\%$; indicating that the sample is a good representation of the population (see Table 11). By inspecting the table of coefficients, the t-test revealed that out of the three predictors, only amotivation was found to be a significant predictor of linguistic factors. Precisely, the t-test revealed that amotivation was a significant negative and medium to large predictor of linguistic factors; $b = -.38$, $\beta = -.48$, t (68) = -4.48, $p < .001$. This indicates that participants who had higher levels of amotivation tended to have lower levels of linguistic factors. However, there were no relations between the predictors intrinsic and extrinsic motivation and linguistic factors. (see Table 12).

Table 10.11
R, R Square, Adjusted R Square

Model	R	R Square	Adjusted R Square	Std. Error of the Estimate	Change Statistics					Durbin-Watson
					R Square Change	F Change	df1	df2	Sig. F Change	
1	.49	.24	.206	.76	.24	7.15	3	68	.000	1.68

Table 10.12
Regression Parameters

Model		B	SE B	β
1	(Constant)	4.30	.73	
	Intrinsic motivation	-.12	.15	-.10
	Extrinsic motivation	.09	.19	.06
	Amotivation	-.38	.09	-.48***

Note: For model 1; $R^2 = .24$, $\Delta R^2 = .034$, * $p < .05$, ** $p < .01$, *** $p < .001$

a- AUB sample

The F-test revealed that the regression model which contained the predictors (intrinsic, extrinsic and amotivation) was not significantly better than the mean in explaining the variance in the outcome variable (linguistic factors), $F(3, 46) = 1.48$, $p = .23$, ns (see Table 13). By inspecting the table of coefficients, although the overall regression model was not significant, the t-test revealed that amotivation was found to be a significant predictor of linguistic factors. Precisely, the t-test revealed that amotivation was a significant negative and medium predictor of linguistic factors; $b = -.35$, $β = -.30$, $t(46) = -2.10$, $p = .041$. This indicates that participants who had higher levels of amotivation tended to have lower levels of linguistic factors. However, there were no relations between the predictors intrinsic and extrinsic motivation and linguistic factors. (see Table 14).

Table 10.13
R, R Square, Adjusted R Square

Model	R	R Square	Adjusted R Square	Std. Error of the Estimate	Change Statistics					Durbin-Watson
					R Square Change	F Change	df1	df2	Sig. F Change	
1	.30	.088	.029	.70	.088	1.48	3	46	.23	1.94

Table 10.14
Regression Parameters

Model		B	SE B	β
1	(Constant)	3.04	1.06	
	Intrinsic motivation	.07	.24	.05
	Extrinsic motivation	.04	.25	.02
	Amotivation	-.35	.17	-.30*

Note: For model 1; $R^2 = .088$, $\Delta R^2 = .059$, * $p < .05$

Regression analysis: predictors of socio-cultural factors

a- UoB sample

The F-test revealed that the regression model which contained the predictors (intrinsic, extrinsic and amotivation) was significantly better than the mean in explaining the variance in the outcome variable (socio-cultural factors), $F (3, 65) = 9.17$, $p < .001$. Moreover, the regression model which contained those predictors explained 29.7% ($R^2 = .297$) of the variance of the outcome variable (socio-cultural factors) at the sample level. The adjusted R square for the regression model was $R^2 adj = .265$, indicating that this regression model explained 26.5% of the variance of the outcome variable (socio-cultural factors) at the level of the population. In addition, when moving from the sample to the population, the shrinkage $\Delta R^2 = 3.2\%$; indicating that the sample is a good representation of the population (see Table 15). By inspecting the table of coefficients, the t-test revealed that out of the three predictors, only amotivation was found to be a significant predictor of socio-cultural factors. Precisely, the t-test revealed that amotivation was a significant negative and medium to large predictor of socio-cultural factors; $b = -.20$, $β = -.40$, $t (65) = -3.82$, $p < .001$. This indicates that participants who had higher levels of amotivation tended to have lower levels of socio-cultural skills. However, there were no relations between the predictors intrinsic and extrinsic motivation and socio-cultural factors. (see Table 16).

Table 10.15
R, R Square, Adjusted R Square

Model	R	R Square	Adjusted R Square	Std. Error of the Estimate	Change Statistics					Durbin-Watson
					R Square Change	F Change	df1	df2	Sig. F Change	
1	.55	.297	.265	.47	.297	9.17	3	65	.000	2.25

Table 10.16
Regression Parameters

Model		B	SE B	β
1	(Constant)	2.41	.47	
	Intrinsic motivation	.17	.09	.22
	Extrinsic motivation	.24	.13	.23
	Amotivation	-.20	.05	-.40***

Note: For model 1; $R^2 = .297$, $\Delta R^2 = .032$, * $p < .05$, ** $p < .01$, *** $p < .001$

b- AUB sample

The F-test revealed that the regression model which contained the predictors (intrinsic, extrinsic and amotivation) was significantly better than the mean in explaining the variance in the outcome variable (socio-cultural factors), $F(3, 46) = 3.60$, $p = .020$. Moreover, the regression model which contained those predictors explained 19% ($R^2 = .19$) of the variance of the outcome variable (socio-cultural factors) at the sample level. The adjusted R square for the regression model was $R^2 adj = .137$, indicating that this regression model explained 13.7% of the variance of the outcome variable (socio-cultural factors) at the level of the population. In addition, when moving from the sample to the population, the shrinkage $\Delta R^2 = 5.3\%$; indicating that the sample is a good representation of the population. (see Table 17). By inspecting the table of coefficients, the t-test revealed that out of the three predictors, only extrinsic motivation was found to be a significant predictor of socio-cultural factors. Precisely, the t-test revealed that extrinsic was a significant positive and medium to large predictor of socio-cultural factors; $b = .47$, $\beta = .42$, $t(46) = 2.82$, $p = .007$. This indicates that participants who had higher levels of extrinsic motivation tended to have lower levels of socio-cultural factors. However, there were no relations between the predictors (intrinsic motivation and amotivation) and socio-cultural factors. (see Table 18).

Table 10.17
R, R Square, Adjusted R Square

Model	R	R Square	Adjusted R Square	Std. Error of the Estimate	Change Statistics					Durbin-Watson
					R Square Change	F Change	df1	df2	Sig. F Change	
1	.44	.19	.137	.46	.19	3.60	3	46	.020	1.84

Table 10.18
Regression Parameters

Model		B	SE B	β
1	(Constant)	1.49	.70	
	Intrinsic motivation	.06	.16	.06
	Extrinsic motivation	.47	.17	.42**
	Amotivation	-.05	.11	-.06

Note: For model 1; $R^2 = .19$, $\Delta R^2 = .053$, ** $p < .01$

Differences between UoB sample and AUB sample on all measures

Normality Analysis

The normality of variables was tested by examining the z-scores of skewness and kurtosis of the variables (intrinsic, extrinsic, amotivation, academic, linguistic and sociocultural factors) across UoB and AUB. The normality analysis revealed that the variable (intrinsic motivation) across UoB had z-skewness scores above the ±1.96 significance level and z-kurtosis scores below the ±1.96 significance level, indicating that intrinsic motivation across UoB was not normally distributed. The normality analysis also revealed that the variable (intrinsic motivation) across AUB had z-skewness scores and z-kurtosis scores below the ±1.96 significance level, indicating that intrinsic motivation across AUB was normally distributed. The normality analysis also revealed that the variable (extrinsic motivation) across UoB had z-skewness scores and z-kurtosis scores below the ±1.96 significance level, indicating that extrinsic motivation across UoB was normally distributed. The normality analysis, however, revealed that variable (extrinsic motivation) across AUB had z-skewness scores above the ±1.96 significance level and z-kurtosis scores below the ±1.96 significance level, indicating that extrinsic motivation across AUB was not normally distributed. The normality analysis also revealed that variable (amotivation) across UoB and AUB had z-skewness scores above the ±1.96 significance level and z-kurtosis scores below the ±1.96 significance level, indicating that amotivation across UoB and AUB universities was not normally distributed. Therefore, three Mann-Whitney U test were conducted to examine the differences between universities on extrinsic, intrinsic and amotivation (see Table 19). The normality analysis also revealed that variables (academic, linguistic, socio-cultural factors) across UoB and AUB had z-skewness scores and z-kurtosis scores below the ±1.96 significance level, indicating that these variables were normally distributed. Since the normality of the variables (academic, linguistic, sociocultural factors) across UoB and AUB was met, then three independent t-tests were conducted to study the differences between universities on academic, linguistic and socio-cultural factors (see Table 20).

Main Analysis

Three Mann-Whitney U tests were conducted to study the differences between UoB and AUB samples on intrinsic, extrinsic and amotivation. The results revealed that AUB students (Mdn = 3.83) had significantly higher levels of intrinsic motivation compared to UoB students (Mdn = 3.5); U = 1162.00, p = .001. Similarly, the results revealed that AUB students (Mdn = 4.25) had significantly higher levels of extrinsic motivation compared to UoB students (Mdn = 4.0); U = 1354.00, p = .020. The results, however, revealed that AUB students (Mdn = 1.25) had significantly lower levels of amotivation compared to UoB students (Mdn = 1.75); U = 1170.00, p = .001 (see Table 19).

Three Independent sample t-tests were conducted to study the differences between UoB sample and AUB sample on academic, linguistic and socio-cultural factors. The results revealed that AUB students (M = 4.08, SD = 0.43) had significantly higher levels of academic skills compared to UoB students (M = 3.60, SD = 0.56); t (118.45) = -5.27, p < .001. The results, however, revealed that AUB students (M = 2.95, SD = 0.71) had significantly lower levels of linguistic skills compared to UoB students (M = 3.45, SD = 0.85); t (120) = 3.39, p = .001. Finally, the results revealed that there were no significant differences between AUB students (M = 3.61, SD = 0.49) and UoB students (M = 3.54, SD = 0.55) on socio-cultural factors; t (117) = 0.75, p = .45, ns (see Table 20)

Table 10.19
Mann-Whitney test

	Intrinsic motivation	Extrinsic motivation	Amotivation
Mann-Whitney U	1162.00	1354.00	1170.00
Wilcoxon	3790.00	3982.00	2445.00
Z	-3.33	-2.33	-3.35
Significance	.001	.020	.001

Table 10.20
Independent sample t-test

	UoB		AUB			
	M	SD	M	SD	t-test	Sig.
Academic factors	3.60	0.56	4.08	0.43	-5.27	.00***
Linguistic factors	3.45	0.85	2.95	0.71	3.39	.00***
Socio-cultural factors	3.54	0.55	3.61	0.49	-0.75	.45

*** $p < .001$

References

Anton, M. 1999. The discourse of a learner-centered classroom: Sociocultural perspectives on teacher-learner interaction in the second-language classroom. *The Modern Language Journal, 83*(3), 303-318.

Baker, J., & Westrup, H. 2003. *Essential speaking skills: A handbook for English language teachers.* London: Continuum.

Banks, J. A., & McGee-Banks, C. 2009. *Multicultural education: Issues and perspectives* (7th ed.). Hoboken, NJ: Wiley.

Brophy, J. E. 1983. Research on the self-fulfilling prophecy and teacher expectations. *Journal of Educational Psychology, 75*(5), 631-661.

Deci, E.L. & Ryan, R.M. 2000. Intrinsic and Extrinsic Motivations: Classic Definitions and New Directions. *Contemporary Educational Psychology, 25*, 54-67.

Dörnyei, Z. 2005. *The psychology of the language learner: Individual differences in second language acquisition.* Mahwah, NJ: Lawrence Erlbaum Associates. Goh, C. C. M. & Burns, A. (2012). *Teaching speaking: A holistic approach.* Cambridge: Cambridge University Press.

Gorham, J. and Christophel, D.M. 1992. Students' perceptions of teacher behaviors as motivating and demotivating factors in college classes. Communication Quarterly, 40, 239-252.
https://doi.org/10.1080/01463379209369839

Harmer, J. 2001. *The practice of English language teaching.* London: Longman.

Horwitz, E.K., Horwitz, M.B. and Cope, J.A. 1986. Foreign Language Classroom Anxiety. The Modern Language Journal, 70, 125-132. http://dx.doi.org/10.1111/j.1540-4781.1986.tb05256.

Lake, V. E., & Pappamihiel, N. E. 2003. Effective practices and principles to support English language learners in the early childhood classroom. Childhood Education, 79(4), 200-204.

Light, G. Cox, R. & Calkins, S. 2009. *Learning and Teaching in Higher Education: The Reflective Professional.* London: Sage Publication.

Luoma, S. 2004. *Assessing speaking.* New York: Cambridge University Press.

Shumin, K. 1997. Factors to consider: Developing adult EFL students' speaking abilities. *English Teaching Forum.* 35 (3), 8. Retrieved from http://eca.state.gov/forum/vols/vol35/no3/p8.htm.

CHAPTER ELEVEN

ESP vs. CLIL in Higher Education

Gabriela Chmelíková, Ľudmila Hurajová

Introduction

The study surveys the common and different features of English for Specific Purposes and Content and Language Integrated Learning and provides a viewpoint on how both approaches can be utilised and implemented in tertiary education. The authors are senior assistants and experienced English language practitioners at the Slovak University of Technology, Faculty of Materials Science and Technology in Trnava, Slovakia and share their results and expertise from their international project titled *Transnational exchange of good CLIL practice among European Educational Institutions* as well as from their institutional project *Research on prerequisites for the internationalisation improvement of the educational environment at STU MTF in Trnava*. At the same time, the authors question the possibilities how, where and to what extent the approaches are/can be implemented in higher education, and in their Faculty, in particular.

There is no doubt that specialists of any kind and particularly those in technology are in high demand, and similarly, nobody questions the fact that the higher the language competence of university graduates the better their skills can be disseminated easily and appropriately. One of the ways to ensure that these future graduates and professionals at engineering universities receive high-quality training is to support their language training.

Regarding the foreign language teaching at the Slovak technical universities, the word of mouth reports from multiple meetings with fellow language teachers and the participation of authors at several international conferences with exchanging experience, the development of language training has probably been similar not only in other Slovak universities but in higher education in other European countries as well. The situation is difficult to understand, as the universities call for internationalisation of their education and would like to attract foreign students, however, in the new accreditation they have lowered their load of lessons in foreign languages teaching. In addition, they dismissed the majority of their language teachers or allotted the rest of them to subject-specific departments. In case of sudden necessity, the universities would rather outsource the lessons and teachers via Language Centres operating for other faculties than utilise the expertise of in-house practitioners – this obviously does not meet the requirement of quality and continuity. At the Slovak University of Technology, Faculty of Materials Science and Technology (hereinafter referred to only as STU MTF), the foreign language teaching was limited just to the English language (from previous four foreign languages variety – English, German, French, and Russian), and the training was lowered from four semesters to two.

All courses at STU MTF in Trnava are built on rigorous needs analysis carried out by experts of the individual Faculty institutes and departments while considering the requirements of the job market and the national/regional needs as well. In addition, regarding the fast technology development, the syllabi are continuously upgraded and innovated. The course in English for Specific Purposes (ESP), titled as English for Science and Technology (EST) focuses primarily on the requirements laid on the STU MTF graduates. The course objective is to teach the students how to manage communication in the English speaking environment, to gain professional competences, to communicate the results achieved both in printed and electronic forms, so that they are able to elicit relevant information, understand presentation, elaborate an individual output and present it in professional events while respecting intercultural differences within EU and other countries and implementing them in negotiations, international conferences and socialising.

What is ESP?

Some of the STU MTF students come across ESP first within the language course which is delivered in the second year of their bachelor study. Sometimes, the teachers have to explain and prepare them for the encounter. Many authors have provided definitions of what ESP (being more specific than LSP – Language for Specific Purposes) is and where it has its place as well. Comparing the approaches of ESP and CLIL, *English for Specific Purposes* came into its existence prior to CLIL, approximately in the 1960s.

Hutchinson and Waters (1993) describe it as a tree "the tree of English Language Teaching/Learning is nourished by its roots which are *learning and communication.*" (p. 16)

As we go up the tree, we can see three branches of English Language Teaching/Learning. One of them is called English as a Foreign Language (EFL). It is divided into two branches:

- General English (GE),
- English for Specific Purposes (ESP) "(Hutchinson, Waters 1993, 16-18).

Nevertheless, the classification goes on further, and we can see other little branches of, e.g. English for Science and Technology (EST), English for Business and Economics (EBE), English for Social Science (ESS).

Robinson (quoted by Dudley-Evans 1998 p. 6), classifies the English language teaching according to the future needs of learners as follows:

- English for Occupational Purposes (EOP)
- English for Academic Purposes (EAP).

What almost all ESP definitions have in common is the fact that ESP is essentially based on needs analysis (Hutchinson and Waters 1987, 53-64), and Dudley-Evans and St. John (1993, p.87), who attributed ESP some characteristics and features:

ESP characteristics:

- Target group – prevailingly intermediate to advanced adult students,
- Used methodologies, activities, and techniques comply with the discipline it serves for,
- Focus on language structures and vocabulary suitable for the target discipline, etc.

ESP features:

- Use of authentic materials (modified by teachers when necessary),
- Encouraging students to search for related materials (supporting thus students' autonomy).

The characteristics and features define the ESP implementation and the situation at STU MTF. Regarding the aforementioned lowered load of the English language training, we try to eliminate the beginners, so that we can work with the materials related to the study programme in question in depth and thoroughly. We also do our best in adopting the methodologies to the target and utilising suitable activities and techniques, e.g., for IT study programmes we use more graphical and schematic materials, for future personnel managers we work with authentic materials selected from regional companies. The same applies to structures, as with IT students we concentrate a little less on oral training as they would not need it to the same extent as say, managers. Regarding the features, for the semester output, the students are encouraged to prepare presentations on a topic of their choice from the materials they find on the Internet.

When speaking about the specific purpose of the lesson, the English practitioners frequently utilise the close cooperation with subject-specific teachers and try to compose their advice and implement the register. The language teachers did their best to understand what is taught by other teachers at the subject-specific departments, research workplaces, in other words, they visited them in their laboratories, tried to comprehend the functions of related equipment, basic operations or technology procedure as then they could refer to real facts within EST training. This does not mean that "the ESP teacher should become a teacher of subject related, but rather an interested student of the subject matter". (Miština 2010, 124) "ESP teachers are professionals and they should also regard their students as professionals, and thus learn from each other". (Dashestani and Stojković 2015, 436).

Compared to CLIL, obviously, within ESP there is content, and although we do not teach solely grammar or vocabulary, we integrate them more or less into the topic dealt with. If necessary, space can be found for a detailed explanation of the structure or register in targeted exercises afterwards.

What is CLIL?

The term Content and Language Integrated Learning (CLIL) has been used for more than a decade in education especially in the field of learning / teaching foreign languages. David Marsh (2002) describes CLIL as situations when subjects or parts of subjects are taught through a foreign language with dual-focused aims: 1) the learning of content and 2) learning of a foreign language – both at the same time. David Graddol (2006) wrote, that "CLIL is an approach to bilingual education in which both curriculum content (such as science or geography) and English are taught together. It differs from simple English-medium education in that the learner is not necessarily expected to have the English proficiency required to cope with the subject before beginning study". Phil Ball (2010) thinks that "If you teach EMI (English as a Medium of Instruction), LAC (Language Across the Curriculum), CBI (Content-based Instruction) or CBLT (Content-based Language Teaching; if you work in Bilingual Education; if you are a subject teacher working through the medium of a foreign language, or a language teacher bringing in content into your English lesson, you work within the area of Content and Language Integrated Learning".

In spite of the fact that there are many definitions of CLIL, they all have one thing in common, CLIL dual learning principle. If teachers consider implementing the CLIL approach, they should be ready to set real CLIL learning environments where students can develop their language competence and content subject knowledge at the same time. As far as the form is concerned, CLIL can be applied either as a CLIL lesson or a CLIL activity within a lesson. In terms of CLIL teachers, they are responsible for setting the dual learning environment, and their qualifications vary.

Within the ERASMUS+ project *Transnational exchange of good CLIL practice among European Educational Institutions*, several approaches regarding CLIL teachers were noticed in four European countries (Latvia, Lithuania, Sweden and Italy). In some cases, FL (foreign language) teachers were in charge of setting the CLIL educational environment, in other cases, a pair of teachers (one FL teacher and another non-language subject teachers), and in the ideal case, in terms of teacher qualification, was a teacher qualified both as a FL teacher and a non-language subject teacher. From a curricular perspective, in some countries CLIL lessons were compulsory and teachers have been trained how to set dual learning environments. Whereas, the schools in other countries have provided just optional CLIL lessons within their curriculum. We also noticed some schools where CLIL lessons were offered as afternoon activities.

One of our project results was finding that there are diverse forms of the CLIL learning environment across Europe based on the educational system set by a particular state. However, there is one aspect that must be followed – the dual learning principle of the CLIL approach.

ESP and CLIL – common features and differences

It is not only the English teachers (or also other foreign language practitioners) who frequently enquire where the ESP stops and CLIL begins. From our point of view, both methodologies are built on the principles of effective learning where all decisions are based on learner´s needs. The common features or differences can be looked and classified at from various aspects. For example, we can mention the following ones: requirements laid on students, requirements laid on teachers, material preparation and its authenticity, background knowledge, language structures, etc.

Regarding several sources (Sobhy, Berzosa and Crean 2013, 256), the essential need here is represented by the ability to transfer knowledge from one area to the other including the transfer of language, i.e., the students as well as the teacher have to have some *background knowledge* when reading a subject-specific article so that they can understand what it is about, and thus can relate what they have read to their own knowledge or schemata. This also means that knowing just the appropriate vocabulary shows to be unsatisfactory. The knowledge can also go deeper, but whether it should be on an ESP or CLIL lesson that is the subject to discussion as this depends on more factors.

The *authenticity of materials* is the other thing ESP and CLIL methodologies have in common. For both, it reads that the more authentic material, the better. In higher education, the students usually work with the materials closely related to their study programmes. Nevertheless, the same authentic material can be processed on a CLIL lesson if it is scaffolded sufficiently. Scaffolding as a technique to get the students closer to the point of the knowledge required or precise meaning is used within ESP lessons as well.

The next feature these approaches have in common is the *register*. The topic related vocabulary can be successfully utilised both in ESP or CLIL lessons by similar (e. g mentioned scaffolding) techniques. The differences between ESP and CLIL methodologies are not numerous. We can find them in using the language *structures* or *the style* as they are not the target within a CLIL lesson, similarly as *the pronunciation* which should be not corrected according to CLIL approach (if it does not interfere the meaning significantly), whereas ESP teachers deal with the language as a complex, including also grammar structures, pronunciation, and style.

Regarding the background knowledge in a CLIL lesson, one might say that it is not necessary to deal with the topic to that extent as in an ESP lesson. Similarly, one could object that the materials could be less authentic (but not necessarily) in a CLIL lesson. However, we think it could be exactly the opposite, and in a CLIL lesson the teacher/learners could deal with the topic in more detail than in an ESP lesson. This depends on many factors. Similarly, the register, in either ESP or CLIL lessons can be the same.

All in all, we can consider both approaches very useful, however, the objective of ESP and CLIL methodologies varies. ESP focuses on known information whereas within CLIL lessons the learners can acquire new information from the related scientific field as well as learn the English language.

CLIL and ESP at Higher Education

As it was illustrated, ESP and CLIL approaches seem to be very similar and it is difficult to find a clear distinction between them. As far as higher education is concerned, teachers can be the distinguishing point applied for recognizing CLIL or ESP regarding their qualifications/specialization. We think that the ESP approach is the FL teacher/expert's domain and non-language subject experts are those ones who can set the CLIL learning environment within their lectures or seminars at universities. Linguistically, English is the widely used foreign language that has been applied to education around the world for a long time. CLIL as an educational approach, aimed at fostering foreign language competence and subject knowledge at the same time, has been mentioned just recently. EMI is more often used to name the process of teaching subjects in English or in another foreign language at universities across Europe, and we think that it reflects the reality. University lecturers, associate professors, and professors, who deliver their courses in English at universities, hardly ever focus on the development of students' English competence. So, when EMI is applied, we think there should be certain requirements on the students' level of English set, as it really is required in almost all such cases.

On the other hand, there is a great pressure on university leaders to internationalize educational environment in higher education to provide an atmosphere for sharing ideas, working on research projects internationally, and enhancing students' and teachers' mobility around Europe and the world.

So, the issue is how to implement English taught courses into accreditation at universities where the majority is represented by students with the same mother tongue and in some cases with a low level of English competence. CLIL might be that solution. CLIL approach provides us many forms how we can start the process of English taught courses implementation. Nevertheless, we think before kicking off the CLIL application some research is needed to gain data for setting the CLIL learning environment tailored to specific university context.

According to McDougald (2017, 12), these areas would provide all practitioners with a starting point to reflect on when considering how to approach language and content in the classroom.

1. **Content area**
   Educators must be well/versed in the particular content subject area that they teach.

2. **Pedagogy**
   Educators must be prepared to implement strategies that provide students with the opportunities to access content in pedagogically valuable ways and employ a range of evaluation options to evaluate both content learning and language learning.

3. **Second Language Acquisition (SLA)**
   Educators need to understand how learner language acquisition develops and evolves over time so as to facilitate the process.

4. **Language teaching**
   Teachers need to know how to support the use and development of the "four skills" (reading, writing, listening, and speaking) of language in their classes.
5. **Materials selection and adaptation**
   Educators must be able to select, and as necessary, adapt a variety of methods, approaches, instructional materials to meet the language/linguistic needs of their students.

We, as ESP experts, have already started working on an institutional research project at our STU MTF. The aim of the project is to investigate: firstly, the teachers' attitude to teaching their subjects in English and their readiness from a linguistic perspective. Secondly, we will study students' attitude and their readiness for the process of smooth CLIL application into education. Thirdly, the phase of the project will be to prepare training for teachers based on foreign language didactics, CLIL methodology, and we also plan to offer some English courses to enhance their development of English competence.

All in all, ESP experts' role at universities in these days can be defined as follows: 1) as facilitators of students' English competence development including the extending of students' specific register in the field their study, 2) as facilitators/supervisors of content subject staff' development in the CLIL approach, SLA area, and foreign language teaching, 3) as supervisors for designing the study materials in English. In this model, there is a shift in ESP teachers' roles and in the qualifications of content subject professionals providing dual learning environment at universities. These should gain new knowledge and skills to become CLIL teachers. This presented model can be just an interim step in the process of implementing English taught courses at universities and lead smoothly to EMI courses or even to the whole study programmes taught in English.

Conclusion

To conclude, the language education at universities is changing; and the documents issued by the European Commission say that the ability to communicate in a foreign language is one of the essential competences not only for mobility, but also for better employability of graduates. Therefore, the solution to the difficult situation at the universities, which are currently suffering from lowering the load of English lessons, could not only be in the close cooperation with subject-specific departments but predominantly in the implementation of the CLIL approach (Hurajová 2015, 106). This was also shown from the good practise experience gained via the international ERASMUS+ project mentioned in the paper and in partial results of the institutional STU

MTF project. These partial results show that this methodology could open new horizons for the tertiary education in the field of foreign language acquisition.

Acknowledgement

This chapter is published as a partial product of the international project ERASMUS+ 2015-1-SK01-KA201-008937 Transnational Exchange of good CLIL practice among European Educational Institutions. The European Commission support for the production of this publication does not constitute an endorsement of the contents which reflects the views only of the author, and the Commission cannot be held responsible for any use which may be made of the information contained therein.

References

Ball, P. *What is CLIL?* accessed 19 March 2018, available online http://www.onestopenglish.com/clil/methodology/articles/article-what-is-clil/500453.article#What%20is%20CLIL

Council of Europe. 2004. *Common European Framework of Reference for Languages: Learning, teaching, assessment.* Cambridge: Cambridge University Press.

Dashtestani., R. and Stojković, N. 2015. "The Use of Technology in English for Specific Purposes (ESP) Instruction: A Literature Review", The Journal of teaching English for Specific and Academic Purposes 3/3. Accessed March 15, 2018. http://espeap.junis.ni.ac.rs/index.php/easpeap_/article/view/304/199

Dudley-Evans, T. and St. John, M. J. 1998. *Developments in English for Specific Purposes. A multi-disciplinary approach.* Cambridge: Cambridge University Press.

Graddol, D. 2006. *English Next*, British Council Publications. Cited in http://www.onestopenglish.com/clil/methodology/articles/article-what-is-clil/500453.article#What%20is%20CLIL

Hurajová, Ľ. 2015. Content and Language - how to integrate them on tertiary level, *R&E source. Special issue 4.* Accessed May 19, 2017 online, 105-108. http://journal.ph-noe.ac.at/index.php/resource/article/view/255/294

Hutchinson, T. and Waters, A. 1993. *English for Specific Purposes: A learning-centered approach.* Cambridge: Cambridge University Press.

Marsh, D. 2002. *CLIL/EMILE – The European Dimension: Actions, Trends & Foresight Potential.* Brussels: European Commission.

McDougald, J. 2017. *Language and content in higher education.* In: Latin American Journal of Content and Language Integrated Learning. 10(1), pp. 9-16. doi: 10.5294/laclil.2017.10.1.1

Miština, J. 2012. *English for academic purposes course design for natural science doctoral candidates.* In: Horváthová, B. et al: New directions in teaching foreign languages. Brno: Masaryk University, pp. 122-137.

Sohby, N., Berzosa, N., and Crean, F. M. 2013. *From ESP to CLIL using Schema Theory.* In: Revista de Lenguas para Fines Especificos, 19, Universidad de San Jorge, pp. 251-267.

Contributors

Anna Stefanwicz-Kocoł (M.A. in English Philology, University of Adam Mickiewicz in Poznan, Poland) is an EFL academic teacher with over 20 years of experience in teaching General and ESP courses. Currently, she is pursuing doctoral research in the field of motivation to learn ESP in a blended learning environment. A college lecturer, she is also an author and co-author of several academic publications in the field of Applied Linguistics and Distance Learning and Teaching, as well as practical teaching materials such as English in Chemistry or Practical Grammar Exercises Part 1and 2. She has also been developing b-learning courses for both General English for Specific Purposes.

Elena Giménez-Forcada (PhD, University of Granada, Spain) is Senior Researcher at Geological Survey of Spain (Instituto Geológico y Minero de España, IGME) where she studies the occurrence and distribution of arsenic in ground waters. She has been an intensive scientific carrier for more than 30 years analyzing the natural quality of groundwater in different geological scenarios, and specifically focusing on the behavior of trace elements. She is the author of numerous scientific publications in this field and has participated in several national and international research projects. She has recently incorporated into her studies the human health factor, developing methodologically her hydro-chemical studies within the new field of Medical Geology. She is currently the leader of the Spanish chapter of the International Medical Geology Association, IMGA-Spain.

Gabriela Chmelíková is a senior assistant at STU MTF in Trnava and Head of the Dpt. of Languages and Humanities. She graduated in Slovak language – English language teaching from the University of Comenius in 1985. In 2008 she received her PhD in linguistics. Gabriela Chmelíková is a member of Slovak Council of CASAJC (Czech-Slovak Association of Language Teachers at Universities), now working as Vice-president. She cooperated on the accreditation file elaboration for UNIcert® II and III levels in English for Engineering Majors in the UNIcert® certification system. In cooperation with colleagues from other departments, she annually organizes Student Research Conference. She has also been involved in several national and international pro-

jects, e.g. "*Student on-line conferences of STU MTF (Slovakia) and University of Niš, Faculty of Electronic Engineering (Serbia) for the purposes of specific English language and other skills development*", or *Transnational exchange of good CLIL practice among European Educational Institutions*", etc.
Her professional interests include ESP, academic skills, pedagogical competences, and the use of multimedia in teaching as well as reading and presentation techniques.

Huang Jian holds a PhD in Applied Linguistics and is an Associate Professor in the School of Foreign Studies, Central University of Finance and Economics. His academic interests cover material development for language and translation instruction and assessment, ESP Teacher development & Qualitative Research.

Iria da Cunha holds a PhD in Applied Linguistics (Universitat Pompeu Fabra, 2008). She is a Ramón y Cajal researcher in the Foreign Languages Department at the Universidad Nacional de Educación a Distancia (UNED) in Spain. She teaches mainly in the areas of Linguistics and Translation. Her main fields of research are Specialized Discourse, Terminology and Natural Language Processing (NLP).

Jorge Diego Sánchez (PhD, Universidad de Salamanca, Spain) is a lecturer at the University of Salamanca (Dpt. of English Studies). He has been teaching ESP courses in International Relations, Medicine and the Arts. His academic research focuses on Postcolonial, Gender and Cultural Studies in English with a focus on literature, cinema and dance from the South Asian Subcontinent and its diaspora. He has completed academic and teaching activities at Trinity College Dublin (Ireland), University of Hyderabad (India) and Jadavpur University (India).

Jungyeon Koo is a PhD student in the department of English Language and Literature at Seoul National University. She is interested in the field of Conversation Analysis, Second Language Acquisition, ESP (English for Specific Purposes), EAP (English for Academic Purposes) and Corpus Linguistics.

Ľudmila Hurajová is a senior assistant in the Department of Languages and Humanities at STU MTF in Trnava. She graduated in Biochemistry from Comenius University in Bratislava, Faculty of Science in 1994 and in English and Literature from Constantine the Philosopher University in Nitra in 2006. In 2013 she received her PhD in English didactics, specifically in CLIL teacher competences. Ľudmila Hurajová is a member of Slovak Council of CASAJC (Czech-Slovak Association of Language Teachers at Universities). In coopera-

tion with colleagues from other departments, she annually organizes Student Research Conference. Currently, she coordinates an ERASMUS+ project *"Transnational exchange of good CLIL practice among European Educational Institutions"* and participates in the international project *"Student on-line conferences of STU MTF (Slovakia) and University of Niš, Faculty of Electronic Engineering (Serbia) for the purposes of specific English language and other skills development"*.
Areas of expertise: English didactics, CLIL methodology, language and pedagogical competences, the use of multimedia in teaching as well as presentation techniques.

M. Angeles Escobar holds a PhD in Linguistics (Utrecht University, 1995). She is Associate Professor in the Foreign Languages Department at the Universidad Nacional de Education a Distancia (UNED) in Spain. She teaches mainly in the areas of Linguistics and English for Specific Purposes. Her main fields of research are First and Second Language Acquisition, English Syntax, and Language for Specific Purposes (LSP).

Miriam Pérez-Veneros holds a PhD in Advanced English Studies from the University of Salamanca (July 2017) and is an associate lecturer at the University of Salamanca, where she teaches courses on syllabus design, the classroom context and English for Specific Purposes (English for International Tourism). Her research focuses on discourse analysis, systemic-functional linguistics and the teaching of English as a second language. In addition, she also works with science popularization articles and their potential application as learning tools in CLIL approaches in different academic settings and with children picture books and their presentation of different family structures and family roles. She has also completed academic activities at the Centre for Language and Communication Research (CLCR) at Cardiff University (Wales).

Monika Pociask has a PhD in the field of Glottodidactics (Applied Linguistics) and works as a teacher of English in the Department of Nursing at the State Higher Vocational School in Tarnów, Poland. Her research interests include specialist languages, English for nurses, evaluation of English course for nurses, developing social competences of nursing students and language learning activities adjusted for the needs of labour market. She is also an author and co-author of several academic publications in the field of Applied Linguistics.

Nadežda Stojković, PhD, Associate Professor, University of Niš, Serbia. She works as a lecturer of English for Specific and Academic Purposes and is the Editor-in-Chief of the Journal of Teaching English for Specific and Academic Purposes, and Advisory Editor for Cambridge Scholars Publishing.

Samar Harkouss, PhD, is a senior lecturer at the American University of Beirut, Lebanon. She has a PhD in Education, specifically, Teaching English as a Foreign Language. She is also the Director of the University Preparatory Program and the University Scholarship Program at AUB. Her research centers on the effect of High Impact Practices on students' success as well as determinants of English as a Foreign Language (EFL) reading comprehension among college-bound learners.

Shi Wenjie is an Associate Professor of TEFL in the School of Foreign Studies, Central University of Finance and Economics, Beijing, China. His research areas are mainly on ESP instruction and assessment.

Svetlana Rubtsova, PhD, Associate Professor, Head of ESP department in economics and law, Dean of the Faculty of Modern Languages at St Petersburg State University, Head of the additional educational program "Translation in the sphere of professional communication", Scientific supervisor of the magistrate program "Modern languages and intercultural communication in the sphere of business and management". Author of papers on translation and ESP teaching, dictionaries and textbooks of Legal English TKT modules 1,2, Certified examiner of BULATS.

Ting-hui Wen, PhD, is an Assistant Professor at the Graduate Institute of Translation and Interpretation, National Changhua University of Education, Taiwan. She has been teaching theories and practices in translation and interpretation to post-graduate students. Her research interests lie in corpus-based translation studies and translator training.

Vanya Katsarska is a senior lecturer at the Aviation Faculty, National Military University, Bulgaria. She has been planning, delivering and assessing the general English and specialized English language courses for BSc cadets and civilian students for many years. She has also been a member of a couple of international groups of ESP teachers, developing and implementing needs-driven ESP courses throughout Europe. Her areas of expertise include ESP curriculum and syllabus development, ESP assessment and aviation English.

Wassim Bekai, PhD, is currently an Assistant Professor at the University of Balamand, Lebanon, and has tutored students from different and diverse academic backgrounds, teaching course units on the structure of English and English as a Foreign Language. His intentions are to continue researching language studies.

www.ingramcontent.com/pod-product-compliance
Lightning Source LLC
Chambersburg PA
CBHW052048300426
44117CB00012B/2025